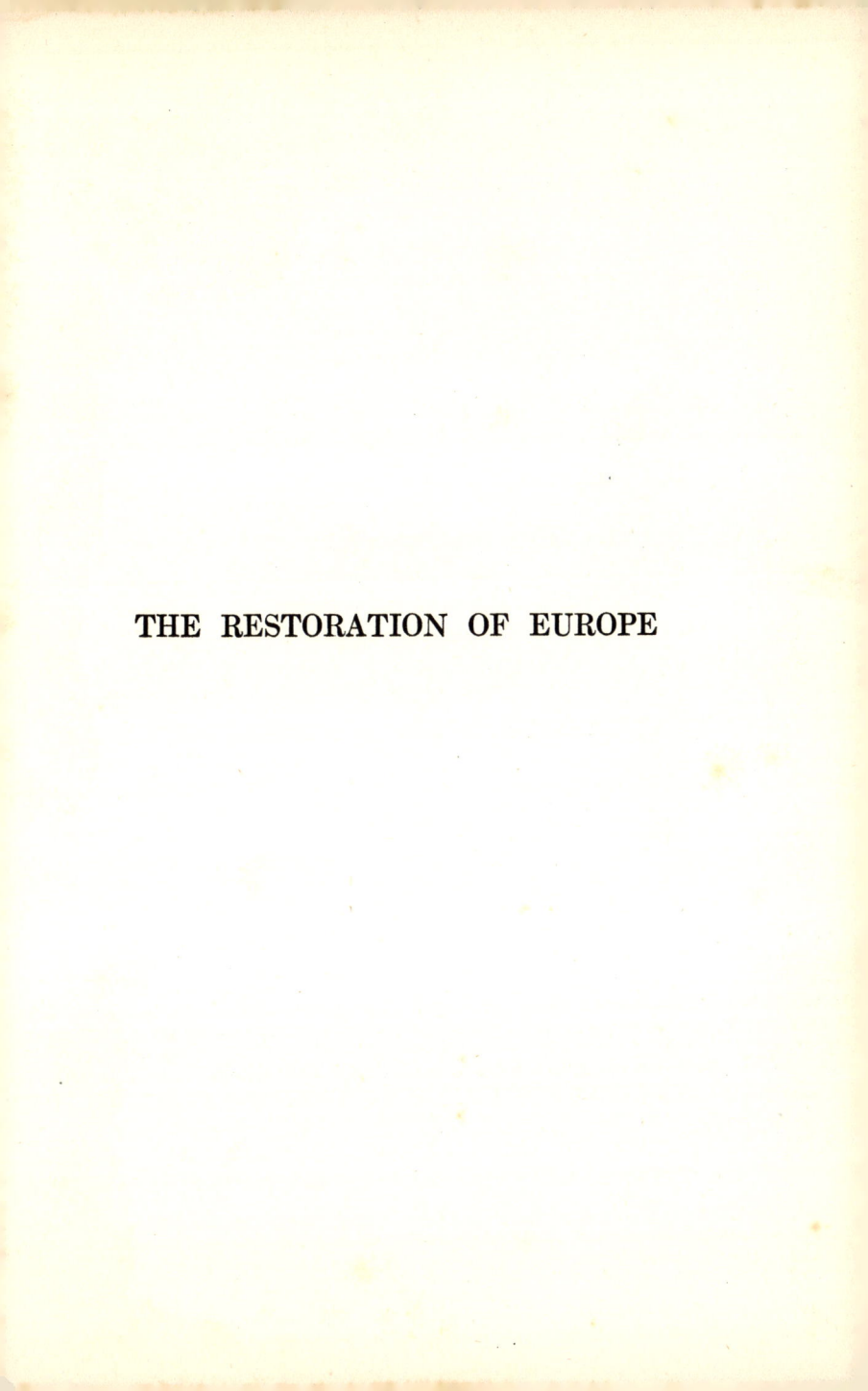

THE RESTORATION OF EUROPE

THE MACMILLAN COMPANY
NEW YORK · BOSTON · CHICAGO · DALLAS
ATLANTA · SAN FRANCISCO

MACMILLAN & CO., Limited
LONDON · BOMBAY · CALCUTTA
MELBOURNE

THE MACMILLAN CO. OF CANADA, Ltd.
TORONTO

THE RESTORATION OF EUROPE

BY

DR. ALFRED H. FRIED

TRANSLATED FROM THE GERMAN
BY
LEWIS STILES GANNETT

New York
THE MACMILLAN COMPANY
1916

All rights reserved

COPYRIGHT, 1916,
BY THE MACMILLAN COMPANY.

Set up and electrotyped. Published May, 1916.

Norwood Press
J. S. Cushing Co. — Berwick & Smith Co.
Norwood, Mass., U.S.A.

TABLE OF CONTENTS

PAGES

CHAPTER I. THE CAUSES OF THE WAR . . . 1–25

It is imperative that representatives of the various nations meet after this world-catastrophe to discuss means of avoiding its repetition. When we distinguish its underlying causes from its immediate occasions, we find that the present war is the logical outcome of the kind of "peace" which preceded it. Although the industrial and technical advances of the last century have made the world interdependent in a sense previously undreamt of, there has been no political adjustment to the changed conditions. More intimate relations gave increasing opportunity for friction, which, so long as the irrational condition of international disorganization persisted, inevitably led to war. War being inevitable, it became the duty of each nation to seize the most favorable moment. The "peace" was really a state of latent and constantly threatening war.

CHAPTER II. THE AGE OF INTERNATIONAL ANARCHY . 26–53

History, from primitive man to Pan-Americanism, is a record of increasing organization. The final step of world-organization will be a product of association rather than of force. Imperialism, supported by the twin fallacies of Mercantilism and Nationalism, is a false philosophy. It defeats its own endeavor to open markets and give nationality free play. It attempts to achieve national security by competitive armament. But the value of armament is purely relative, and every nation cannot have an armament superior to that of every other. The armament system has indeed led to the system of alliances, a valuable if partial form of association. The fact that this war could not be localized demonstrates the real interdependence of the world. Pacifism would achieve national security by realizing this interdependence in political and economic association. The Hague Conferences have made a significant beginning. But international relations must be changed before their work can be effective. The evolution toward internationalism has been further evident in the increasing number of general international treaties regulating economic and social matters. The war has demonstrated the necessity of continuing that evolution out of international anarchy into international organization.

CHAPTER III. THE WAR'S LESSONS UP TO DATE . 54–84

The war has demonstrated that armaments are a symptom of international anarchy and cannot insure peace. The cause must be attacked. By their intense sensitivity, armaments have actually become a menace. Dilatory treatment of international disputes — such as is provided for in the Bryan treaties — will usually obviate war. But the mere provision of such machinery without the will to use it, is inadequate.

The war has demonstrated that attempts to humanize war are futile because self-contradictory. War suspends morality, and cannot be regulated. This war has been more cruel than past wars not because men have been more cruel, but because its area has been so vast and its battlefield so highly civilized. The Hague Conventions, by their qualifications, recognize their own futility.

The war has further demonstrated the futility of war as a political instrument, and destroyed the magic of military romance.

Finally, it seems to confirm the prophecy of Jean Bloch that a modern world-war would be so tremendous that it could only end in exhaustion, and could hardly lead to any decisive result.

TABLE OF CONTENTS

CHAPTER IV. THE TREATY OF PEACE AND FUTURE
PEACE 85–101

This war really began decades ago. What we called "peace" was latent war. The treaty of peace must establish a durable peace. All the nations are supposedly fighting for a "lasting peace" — not realizing that there is no such thing as a lasting peace maintained by force. Peace must be coöperative. The old status of perpetual fear and insecurity, defended only by armaments, would be intolerable. A different system must be established. There might well be two conferences after the war — one to attend to the mere cessation of hostilities, the other to lay the foundations of a new European organization. In this last the neutrals would join.

CHAPTER V. INTERNATIONAL PROBLEMS . . . 102–133

The pacifist movement suffers from Utopians who fail to realize that social evolution is not mechanical but organic.

The organization of nations need not be compulsory, but should rest upon the interest which the individual states have in coöperation.

Secret diplomacy and its elaborate etiquette are outgrown and have become dangerous. An antiquated conception of sovereignty is one of its most dangerous idols. Diplomacy should be democratized.

The system of alliances (balance of power) avoided some wars, but it nourished suspicion and distrust, and thus enhanced the ultimate danger of war. A general European alliance would give real security.

There must be a reduction of armament. This cannot occur unless the danger of surprise attack is eliminated by some method of international control. The armament trade should be nationalized.

The jingo press is one of the worst dangers of the age, deliberately inciting to war. It must be regulated — and chiefly by public opinion.

Hate, the atmosphere which justifies the methods of force, must be done away with. It is not a political reality, nor has it ever been so permanent as we are prone to imagine.

CHAPTER VI. THE COÖPERATIVE UNION OF EUROPE . 134–145

There is no need of political federation. The bonds of self-interest may be strengthened by economic association in a Coöperative Union. The Pan-American Union and the Pan-American Bureau are valuable precedents. Unless Europe so organize herself, America will win an irretrievable advantage. Eventually such a Union would react upon political life, and a World-Union would be the final result.

CHAPTER VII. THE PACIFISM OF YESTERDAY AND OF
TO-MORROW 146–157

The titles of Kant's "Eternal Peace" and Bertha von Suttner's "Lay Down Your Arms" have never represented the programme of pacifists, but they have led to much misunderstanding. Pacifists maintain that wars are inevitable so long as international anarchy persists. They foresaw the present war. Nor has pacifism been without its effect upon scientific and popular thought. The future is in our hands. It is for us to determine whether it shall be a reversion to barbarism or an era of restoration.

AUTHOR'S FOREWORD TO THE AMERICAN EDITION

MY DEAR MR. GANNETT: —

From the little book of mine which you are presenting in English translation to the American public you have learned how significant for unfortunate Europe I believe the example of fortunate America to be. I see in the noble achievement of the Pan-American Union the example of organization which the European nations must follow if they wish to avoid in the future such catastrophes as that to which they are now fallen a sacrifice.

I am therefore very glad that you are presenting my little book to the reading public of America. Perhaps it will help it to realize the great duty which, after the war, you Americans will have to fulfil toward us Europeans. Perhaps the Americans will see how urgent is their call to assist in the task of restoring our continent. America's interests too are at stake. For if we in Europe do not succeed in following the American example, there will be danger that the European example may be followed in America. All friends of Humanity must strive to guard the world from this danger.

I am, respectfully yours,

Dr. Alfred H. Fried.

Berne, February 24, 1916.

TRANSLATOR'S FOREWORD

ALFRED H. FRIED was born in Vienna, Austria, in 1864, lived for many years in Berlin, and now makes his home in Berne, Switzerland. His interest in international problems has been lifelong. For decades he has been attacking mediævalism and militarism in the German and Austrian Empires. Twenty-five years ago he helped form the German Peace Society. For fifteen years he published the "Friedens-Warte" (Watch-tower of Peace) in Berlin, and since the war he has continued its publication in Zurich. Baroness Bertha von Suttner, author of "Lay Down Your Arms," a book which was said to have stimulated the Czar to call the first Hague Conference, was his intimate friend and a regular contributor to the "Friedens-Warte." In 1894 he translated into German the Russian sociologist Novicow's little masterpiece, "War and its Alleged Benefits," and in 1915, after the outbreak of the war, he brought out a second edition of it. A number of other translations and over a score of books stand to his credit, among the latter being a "Handbuch der Friedensbewegung" (1905, 2d edition 1911), "Pan-Amerika" (1910) and "Der Kaiser und die Weltfriede" (1910). "The Restoration of Europe" was published in April, 1915. In 1911 he was awarded the Nobel Peace Prize, and in 1913 the University of Leyden, Holland, gave him the honorary degree of Doctor of Political Science.

What Germans will think about the problem of War and Peace is of tremendous significance to the world. So long as we lay the entire blame for the war on either one of the leading belligerents, so long as we see a solution in the humiliation of one or the crushing of the other — so long true peace is impossible. The elimination of no single nation as a factor in international affairs will solve the world-problem. The disease is not national; it is international. The task that will confront the world can never be achieved by one group of allies or in a spirit of hate — it must be a product of international coöperation.

Dr. Fried represents a wing of German thought which had been gaining in influence, and which will profit by the revulsion of feeling that will inevitably follow the war. (The author of "J'Accuse" is one of those who had come under his influence.) Dr. Fried speaks as a German thinking internationally, never as a pro-German. He nowhere condones in Germany what he condemns in other nations; he never seeks excuses — he seeks causes.

Dr. Fried does not offer us a panacea to abolish war. He knows there is no panacea. The fundamental problem is for nations to learn to coöperate in little things — and in bigger and bigger things. But the core of the matter is to get the will of the world behind international coöperation. To create this will is the great task of education before us. As Dr. Fried says, "A beautiful treaty for world-organization could be made in twenty-four hours, if only the will were there to give it life and to enforce it."

The present situation is intolerable. A nation is unsafe if unprepared. It is prepared only if it has a navy stronger than that of some other nation or nations. It feels unsafe if they are stronger. Human nature being human nature, these others will feel unsafe if it is stronger. They will prepare more in order to achieve safety as they see it. Preparedness means competitive preparedness; and ultimately, inevitably, that means war. Europe has taught us that. Yet a nation is unsafe if unprepared. This is the dilemma in which present-day international anarchy leaves us.

What are we going to do about it? Sit by and accept wars as eternally and constantly inevitable? That is not the American way. Americans admit difficulties, but they face them. So does Dr. Fried.

L. S. G.

The translator's thanks are due to Dr. John Mez for assistance and suggestions in making this translation.

THE RESTORATION OF EUROPE

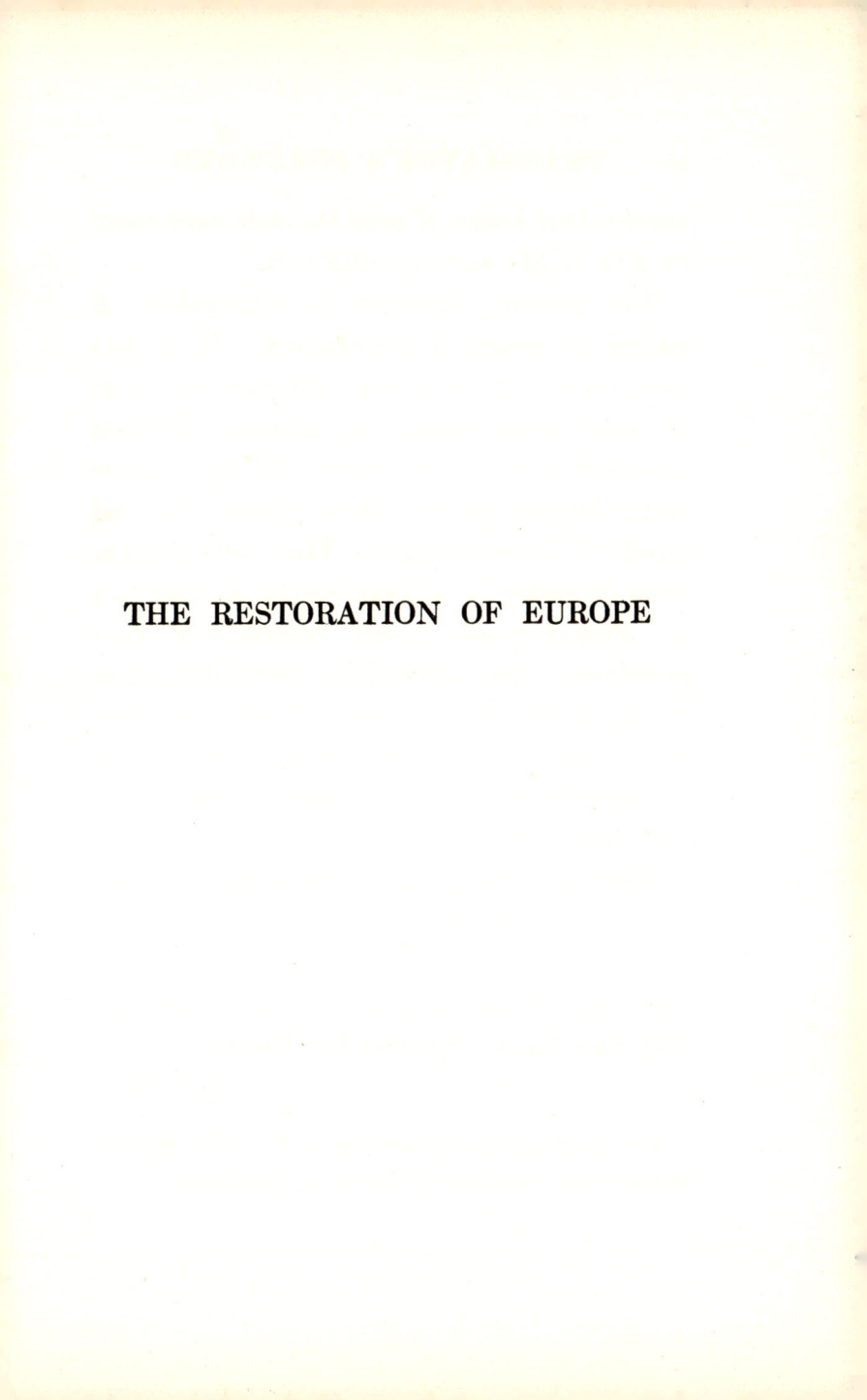

THE RESTORATION OF EUROPE

CHAPTER I

THE CAUSES OF THE WAR

WHEN the *Titanic* sank in April, 1912, our minds were still functioning normally and sanely; to all of us it seemed a disaster that two thousand human beings should be killed by the whim of an iceberg. Sorrow and sympathy were not yet limited by national boundary-lines. As a logical consequence of so vast a disaster, and of the emotions which it had so deeply stirred, a conference of all the seafaring nations was called to devise means of preventing the repetition of such an accident.

When Europe awakens from the convulsions of this war, human life and human happiness, the rights of property and the dignity of labor, will regain their former status. Just in proportion as the sacrifices have been greater and the destruction more terrible, will the reaction from this world-war be more certain. None but prating fools presume to glorify it. As after the shipwreck, men will consider how the repetition of so horrible an experience may be avoided. We would not be men if we did otherwise. Our minds are not so tragically primitive that we who know the lesser evil to be a preventable accident, would accept the incomparably greater as Fate, inevitable, and to be accepted with resignation.

When this continental earthquake, felt the world around, unparalleled in history, involving the destruction of a whole flourishing generation, this cosmic spasm without precedent in the past, is at last happily at an end, millions and millions of men resolved and eager to do so, will be free to undertake the restoration of Europe. Theirs will not be the task of a day. Those who are now in the prime of their powers will give their whole lives to

THE CAUSES OF THE WAR

it, and those who are children to-day will hardly see its completion. For the rest of us, we who up to the summer of 1914 enjoyed the glowing pageant of life and dared hope to behold the fulfilment of the old order of civilization, for us the world, during this period of reconstruction after the war, will be like a vast work-yard, with whose scaffoldings, rubbish-heaps and piles of material, with whose disorder and disquiet we will have to put up, as long as we live. No mere recovering of shattered roofs, no mere re-erecting and repainting of façades, will be enough. The foundation was rotten, and that was what caused the catastrophe.

This task of restoration must be undertaken at the same time everywhere, and from the very beginning the coöperation of all the nations must be sought. They will have to agree upon the general outline of the plans. The details will take care of themselves. As after the *Titanic* disaster, representatives of the various governments will be called together to determine the best means of avoiding another catastrophe like that of 1914–15. The one aim of the work must be the protection of the future.

Civilization rests upon the ability of the human intellect to profit from experience. The operation of the complicated apparatus of daily life is made possible by the myriad experiences of the past. And the future may reach a higher level only because each day puts new experiences at its service. We will emerge from this fearful catastrophe, with all its sorrow and misery, richer in experience. It is not to be imagined that we will apply it only in the science of ordnance. *We must not allow military sciences to be the only ones to profit by these achievements of human thought.* In the midst of this bloody struggle, many have ceased to think of anything else; but mankind has other spheres of activity very close to its heart, and when the agony is over, these other interests will make themselves felt with such primitive force that the threatening artillery-spirit will no longer predominate. The world-war must be utilized by the future in other ways — above all else, to teach us how to prevent repetition of such a catastrophe.

Humanity would not be worthy of its name if, after all these sinister experiences, it did not seriously inquire how such horrors were possible, what circumstances contributed to such a consummation, how they can be avoided in the future, and why such preventive agencies as were already established, failed. In the days of so-called "peace" we did not heed the voice of warning, but allowed ourselves to be misled by fools into believing that wars were natural phenomena, similar to earthquakes and thunderstorms. Now that war has seized the very citadel of civilization we will never again allow ourselves to be so easily deceived. We are approaching an unprecedented period of criticism, very different from, and superior to, the old scepticism. Mankind, especially in Europe, will undertake a fundamental investigation of these things, and will not cease enlightening itself. The time for intellectual jugglers and tight-rope walkers is past. We will no longer allow ourselves to be deceived by simple tricks and intellectual sleight-of-hand. The spectre of the millions slain, the presence of the million cripples, the smoking ruins of the towns and cities and the broken links of commerce will form a picture in whose frame only men who seek and tell the hard unvarnished truth can hold a place. They alone will be recognized as able to utilize the lessons of the war for the service of the future. Only earnest students of fact will be able to determine the causes of this catastrophe, and to demonstrate how its repetition may be avoided.

In analyzing the real causes of this war, we must not be content to discover its immediate occasions. *Cause and occasion are two different things.* What we saw developing in those eleven historic days (July 25 to August 4, 1914) was only the last phase of a process that had long been maturing. Short-sighted people see the beginning of the conflict in what was rather its final phase, and

THE CAUSES OF THE WAR

delude themselves with the naïve belief that Europe is burning and bleeding because Serbia would not permit the participation of an Austro-Hungarian official in a judicial investigation, or that the world-war is only an accidentally enlarged punitive expedition for the crime of Serajevo. There are some already who realize that this conception is too naïve, and seek for deeper motives. Every day new underlying causes of the war are discovered and displayed — which sufficiently proves that imaginations are awake, although there is very little probability to support most of these hypotheses. There can be only one cause, and we are offered a thousand. Such richness is evidence of false thinking. There are too many who seek, not to investigate facts, but to expound, or sometimes to propound, a theory.

Since we regard *the events of those eleven days* as simply phenomena attendant upon the occasion of the war, we need not trouble to discuss them here. Not that such discussion is insignificant — on the contrary, those diplomatic proceedings possess symptomatic importance as showing the absurdity of the system which gave rise to them. They demonstrate its perversity and imbecility. But I do not think the time has yet come when we can discuss them without prejudice. All the official collections of diplomatic papers make the same mistake. They all prove the absolute fairness and infallibility of one side, and impose the full burden of guilt upon the other. An impartial reader of these varicolored books might form a judgment from them to-day. But who is there in Europe to-day who is impartial? Thorough and unbiassed international discussion and objective study will be necessary before any authoritative conclusion can be reached.

Even were this possible, we would not thereby have achieved our real purpose. We might learn what rôles the individual governments played, might survey the actions of individual statesmen, know who at the last moment tried to postpone the war, and who precipitated it; but we would still lack

THE CAUSES OF THE WAR

insight into the motives that influenced the action of the governments, and at a given moment made a given course inevitable. Only when we understand the impersonal elements in this catastrophe, shall we be able to solve the problem of the future.

He who has faith in the human race and believes in human progress, may derive some comfort and consolation from an investigation into these deeper and more impersonal causes. He is spared the shame and horror of believing that a few individuals planned and caused this world-massacre. In perspective we realize that these unfortunates were pulled by unseen strings, that *they were led and not the leaders*, and we rejoice, not so much because they are personally absolved, as because humanity is thereby acquitted of the charge of having given birth to such monsters in human countenance. In this sense it is a service to humanity to turn from the immediate occasions to an investigation of the deeper causes of the world-war.

Pacifists, who long ago recognized these

deeper causes, who prophesied the impending catastrophe and showed how it might have been avoided, have no difficulty in pointing out the ultimate causes of the present massacre.

We can put it very briefly: *The present war is the logical outcome of the kind of "peace" which preceded it.*

Was it really a condition of peace that came to an end in those July days of 1914?

We must recall the political situation that gave rise to the catastrophe in order to answer this question and to understand the connection of the war with that "peace."

"War is as old as man," we are told. The prophets of eternal war are so far right. But when they begin to shape the future according to the moulds of the past, they leave logic behind. Human nature changes, institutions change, even war changes. These changes produce various results. The relation of the state to war has changed much in the last century. Formerly when a war came to an end, the warring nations entered upon a real peace. The economically inde-

THE CAUSES OF THE WAR 11

pendent state recovered in time of peace the condition of order necessary for its continued existence. (After all, peace and order are essentially synonymous.) International contacts were not yet developed — they occurred only in war-time. Peace as yet was uninfluenced by them.

But in the last century the world has completely changed. Something that stands above and between the nations has been evolved. The State is no longer an independent organism. The rapid development of science and industry has begun to weld the states into a complex organism, and to make the formerly independent and self-sufficient units, parts of a higher whole. I know how sceptical some people are to-day in regard to this so-called internationalism. But there is as little reason to believe this movement ended as to fancy that a winter forest has lost its capacity to leaf and blossom. We are dealing with facts. The revolutionary changes in the technical sciences have contracted the world to a degree of which even recent generations never dreamed. Men and nations are at each other's doors. All the peoples of the earth have become interdependent. He who does not see this to-day, when the war has upset the entire life of the world, must be blind. There is interdependence in material and in spiritual life, in production and exchange, in ideas; even emotions and sensations have become internationalized. The interests of society have become common to such a degree that they can be prosecuted and regulated effectively only by the commonwealth of nations. In countless fields an international and often world-wide coöperation is already successfully established. A tendency toward "symbiosis" has asserted itself with the force of a natural law.

Meanwhile the political relations of nations and the spirit in which they are conducted have not kept pace with this mighty force which the progress of industry has called forth and is daily strengthening. Life has an entirely new orientation. But while the conditions of actual life have presented a picture of ever-increasing coöperation, order and organization, international relations have been conducted according to principles preserved from the era of complete isolation and self-sufficiency.

Hence that terrible *discord* which is the great evil of our age.

The nations did not yet realize their actual community of interest. Their myriad interests spread like a network over the entire earth, the farthest corners of which had been brought close to them by the development of industry and transportation. It was but natural that the opportunities for friction were thereby increased, that conflicts of interest, which had formerly been few and isolated, came to be of daily occurrence. The evil lay, not in the new conditions of the time, but in the neglect of political adjustment to these conditions, in the conflict between the tendency to interdependence and the old system of force. Friction occurred because of insufficient adjustment to the new conditions of life; it might have been removed by heeding the world-demand for organization. It arose only because there lingered the tradition of independent action instead of coöperation, because instead of international organization, *international anarchy* had developed. The error was ours; it was not inherent in the nature of things.

With the progress of industry and science in the last generation, this international anarchy increased enormously. As interdependence and the struggle for power among men simultaneously developed, the conflict deepened. The national isolation produced in the normal relations between nations an antagonism as sharp and bitter, and as effective of evil, as had been produced by the wars of the past. It was even worse than before.

Civilized society — at least as far as the leading states of Europe were concerned — ceased waging war. Wars occurred only on the peripheries of civilization. But for a long time the nations had not been living in real peace. They were not nominally at war, and they appeared to be at peace, but in reality the condition was one of latent war, differing from acute war, where the guns are actually fired, *only in degree and not in kind*. Because the tools of war were at rest, because the swords did not clash nor the cannon thunder, men had come to believe that they lived in a society which could dispense with force. As a matter of fact, force controlled the situation, and arms, without actually coming into service, decided the course of events.

For three decades European society had, without realizing it, lived in this condition, had been controlled by it, had grown into it. And this condition was called peace, because in days gone by, real peace had followed when wars were at an end. Peace is essentially order and organization. But organization within the individual states was no longer sufficient; it had become equally necessary in the relations between states. There organization was lacking, and hence there could be no true peace. *It was really latent war*, awaiting only the occasion to become acute.

That is why I said that this war in which we are to-day engulfed is *the logical outcome of the kind of "peace" which preceded it.* We did not have true peace. What we are experiencing with horror to-day is only the conclusion of a process to which the present generation had become accustomed, the inevitable outcome of that condition of latent war which grew out of the lack of human adjustment to the natural course of evolution, and made anarchy dominant.

Once we realize the essential identity of war and such "peace," once we understand that the present war is but the logical outcome of such "peace," then we approach the fundamental causes of the world-war.

Pacifism, which public opinion, with amusing naïveté, has declared a failure, because the outbreak of hostilities supposedly refuted its teachings, has in reality been fully justified by the war. Because we saw that war was bound to result from this condition of national isolation, we worked, warned and sought to develop the forces of organization as a preventive. We had no illusions; we were engaged in the struggle against a catastrophe which we clearly foresaw, when it broke upon us. We never doubted that the opposing forces were stronger. Just because we knew them to be stronger, we tried to strengthen the forces working for order.

We saw the war coming. In an article published in 1908 entitled "The Foundations of Revolutionary (*i.e.*, Constructive) Pacifism," I pointed out that "in this condition (of anarchy and isolation) each nation must count every other its enemy, every advance of one people means disaster for another, the welfare of one the loss of another. All forces work against each other, and out of the confusion there is *often no way of escape except explosion, no salvation except through the catastrophe of war*. War may thus be a necessity because it liberates, because it eliminates conditions which have become intolerable, because it makes a way out; in this case war means liberation and is actually rational. This, however, implies that war is only *so long* a necessity, *so long* a liberating force, *so long* a rational recourse, *as the conditions which produce it are irrational.* It does liberate when the nations have found no escape through reason from the abnormal conditions in which they are living to-day. It is necessary as long as irrationality hampers the normal development of life. . . . *War is rational only as long as the conditions of international society are irrational.*" I further pointed out that the spontaneous explosion of accumulated tension-forces was no longer the greatest danger, since the forces of increasing organization were already working toward an equilibrium. To me the real peril lay in the fact that "the men who conduct the affairs of state, not recognizing this process, *might still fear an explosion and therefore might deliberately attempt to anticipate it. The fear of being suffocated in the prevailing international anarchy is the chief cause of war to-day.* For in this condition of disorder the normal activity or development of one state threatens another with loss of breathing space and elbow-room. Naturally this other state, anxious for its own future, or fearing that its own normal development will be hampered, will deliberately *make war* before it comes to spontaneous explosion, *in the hope that by deliberate aggression, by seizing the opportune moment, it may create conditions favorable to itself in the conflict.*"

This characterization of European conditions was written seven years ago, immediately after the second Hague Conference. We pacifists, therefore, can hardly be accused of having been misled by illusions or surprised by the events of the summer of 1914. On the contrary, things have taken exactly the course which our understanding of the causes had led us to fear. We differ from others only in that we sought out and pointed out by what means the calamity might have been avoided. But our efforts did not have the success they merited. The forces working for organization, which we had awakened and unceasingly sought to strengthen, were too weak; and so, as we had predicted, the explosion came. Let us therefore repeat: *This world-war is the logical outcome of the kind of peace which preceded it.* Its ultimate causes are not to be found in the plans or intrigues of individual governments or diplomats, but in that *state of international anarchy* which determined their plans and intrigues, and which finally reached a moment of tension when explosion was inevitable.

Although the sins of European diplomacy in those eleven days were many, and although a little more determination might have prevented this war, just as worse crises had been passed in recent years, we must admit that many of the negotiations which without this insight into their deeper motives appear incomprehensible and almost criminal, are thus quite explicable.

European diplomacy in the summer of 1914 was not guided by the thought of any form of European federation. It was only too far removed from the condition of international organization which, in the article written in 1908 to which I have already referred, I defined as a system of economic forces in which "the parts combine in a higher whole, the organs unite to form an organism, and the forces work together for mediation and *coöperation.*" Nothing like that existed last summer. European diplomacy was entirely under the influence of that international anarchy described above, in which "every advance of one people means disaster for another," in which explosion seems a blessed relief from tension, and in which it may appear wise precaution to cause such an explosion by deliberate aggression.

Thus we can readily understand how the Austro-Hungarian monarchy saw a danger to its own vital interests in the struggle for national expansion on the part of its southern neighbor. It feared the seizure of some of its own territory and the loss of some of its population. In view of the entire lack of international organization in Europe, we can perhaps understand the Austrian severity of procedure and her refusal to accept any proposals of mediation — all the more when we remember that the dogma of the supposed imminent decline of the Habsburg monarchy made it imperative for her to show vigorous signs of life.

But we can also understand that the same disorganization which led Austria-Hungary to adopt such a course, made it equally necessary for Russia to regard the success of such a policy as a threat to herself. Since in this anarchy "the advance of one people means disaster for another," the success of Austria-Hungary on the Balkan Peninsula necessarily — always from the point of view of the international anarchy — implied defeat for Russia. We can also understand that Germany must fear, in a defeat of her ally by Russia, a defeat for herself. And finally England's attitude can be explained on the same principle — a German defeat of Russia and France would have to be conceived as defeat for England.

THE CAUSES OF THE WAR

If the prevailing international disorganization explains the confused character of the negotiations, it also explains *why they were so hurried — and it was really this hurry which rendered futile the opposing stand of the forces for peace.* The disorganized state of affairs was unquestionably the cause of that over-armament which was supposed to be the only protection against the catastrophe. Unfortunately, the world-catastrophe was required to prove that this idea of defence was illusory, as indeed all reasoning based on anarchy must be. The armaments themselves made the collapse inevitable. Their steady increase made them more and more sensitive. Their effectiveness could be distinctly increased by redistributions and improvements in the system of transportation. Finally this alleged "guarantee of peace," in logical demonstration of its unfitness, became so extremely sensitive that a start of only twenty-four hours in the mobilization of one state appeared an irretrievable disadvantage to the other. The same international anarchy explains Germany's twelve-hour ultimatum to Russia, with all its fearful consequences.

We can understand now why the measures rushed through because of this disorganization led the German government to suspect that these hurried proceedings were only the last steps in a plot to strangle her, so that she found herself in the position I have described where "a state, anxious for its own future, fearing that its own normal development will be hampered, will deliberately make war before it comes to spontaneous explosion, in the hope that by deliberate aggression, by seizing the opportune moment, it may create conditions favorable to itself in the conflict." We may grant that Edward VII sincerely strove to establish European peace upon a firmer basis; and yet, in view of the prevailing international disorganization, we cannot blame the German statesmen if they considered the fulfilment of his desires a menace to Germany, increasing the danger of her loss of "breathing-space and elbow-room."

This explains many of the negotiations and decisions of those unhappy eleven days. Of course it does not justify them. He who is convinced that health and salvation can come to this suffering continent only through world-organization, and who believes such organization already possible, must regard those actions — unless so explained — as criminal madness. But he must admit that the international anarchy with its false assumptions did lead inevitably to the dangerous ideas, conclusions and actions which determined the attitude of statesmen, and were the underlying causes of the world-war.

CHAPTER II

THE AGE OF INTERNATIONAL ANARCHY

THE fanatics of force deny that the process of international organization is approaching its realization and that there exists a natural tendency to coöperation. They justify their attitude with all sorts of arguments based upon their own peculiar philosophy. They *mechanize the teachings of history* — they would conduct the affairs of to-day according to precepts handed down from the time of Charlemagne. But the right of the past can no longer be right in a present that is completely changed. The change has been so unprecedentedly rapid and revolutionary that the militarists cannot realize that not even the immediate past can give us rules of action for the present. Psychologically and technologically, even the age of Bismarck lies far behind us.

They see in history nothing but the decisions of force, entirely overlooking the fact that the whole course of world-history is a process of constantly increasing organization, that an uninterrupted line of progress leads *from isolated primitive man up to modern Pan-Americanism.* They do not realize that this evolution of the human race in history is simply the expression of a universal natural law that leads from chaos to world-organization as from cell to Homo Sapiens. Evolution is always the outcome of association and organization.

But even those who begin to understand this process, and modify their philosophy accordingly, attempt to prove that the various steps toward organization in the past could not have been taken without the use of force. They conclude that future progress in human organization can take place only by war and subjugation. To the creation of the world-state they would apply the experiences of the age when nations were in the making, entirely neglecting the changed conditions and the difference in purpose. Even the methods of nation-building have been modified. The crude method of subjugation is replaced in modern history by such federative association as we see in the United States of America or in the German Empire. Why should the world-state, *i.e.*, the political adaptation of all the nations to the world-tendency towards interdependence, be created by that most impractical method, subjugation — especially when the conditions have so entirely changed? Here the method of subjugation, commonly known as Imperialism,[1] is futile. For it is based on the attempt to assure the world-interests of the individual state, and upon the will of each state to maintain itself in the world-competition. Imperialism attempts to achieve its aims clumsily, by a policy of force, with the desire to reap for a single state all the benefits of world-organization. It would impose order upon the world instead of attaining it by mutual

[1] Dr. John Mez suggests that perhaps Dr. Fried consistently uses the word *Imperialismus* instead of *Militarismus* because of the censorship. — TR.

agreement. The method of force must necessarily come to grief because the different Imperialist ambitions conflict, and hence it hinders rather than helps the development of the desired order and stability. Ultimately the nations will have to come to an agreement. For Imperialism means not only the will to world-power on the part of one state, but the firm and united opposition of all the other states which are thereby menaced. The only way in which it can work toward organization is by organizing opposition. A united opposition will arise against any state whose Imperialist policy menaces other states. It will play the part of the nucleus whose friction organizes the cell.

The fallacy of Imperialism is shown by its very foundations — Mercantilism and Nationalism.

The advocates of force justify their methods by pointing out the necessity of providing markets for home products. But this necessity results from the lack of world-organization and the consequent attempt of each state to assure these conditions of life for itself alone, without consideration of the vital rights of others. When political organization of the world shall open its markets to all the members of the world-state, there will no longer be any necessity for their violent appropriation by any one member. Thus Imperialism is compelled to advocate force for a goal which could be attained without force were it not that Imperialism itself prevents such organization. Such a circle of errors is evidence of the unfitness of the method.

It is in commerce, in the exchange of goods (the most conspicuous characteristic of modern organization), that international interdependence is most obvious. Thanks to our intellectual progress as expressed in industrial and technical development, we are to-day in a position to use the products of the entire earth in any part of the earth and to put the highest products of technical skill and adaptation in any one place to service in all other places. World-commerce makes the technical skill which centuries have developed in any one part of the earth serviceable in all other regions. To manufacture goods may take a long time, but by modern methods of transportation they are rapidly distributed, even to those who have given no time to their production. By exchange we anticipate our own development. What a tremendous factor for organization! With its aid we transcend thousands of miles, and centuries as well — both space and time.

But this exchange of goods brings with it not only friendly relations and contacts, but friction as well — more and greater friction than when nations were more isolated. What does the Imperialist conclude? That commerce is not an agency for peace but a cause of war! It is the false conclusion of the near-sighted. War is not caused by commerce, but by *the maladaptation of political relations to the new conditions created by world-commerce*. Commerce has increased and extended the contacts and relationships — and these require organization far more than ever before. Given world-organization, the friction would cease, or, if it continued, it would be settled not by armed conflict but by treaty. Imperialism justifies itself by the alleged inevitability of war on account of these commercial conflicts. What they really demonstrate is the irrationality and harmfulness of Imperialism.

The other false buttress of Imperialism is Nationalism. As in Mercantilism, so in Nationalism, Imperialism perpetuates an evil, which it alone makes an evil.

The individual states were established by Nationalism. But because Nationalism has the peculiarity of undermining the inner life of nations and of developing embittered antagonisms between nations, it is one of the chief hindrances to internationalism. Essentially it too is characterized by a desire for association, but for a too limited form of association. It emphasizes certain superficialities, which it misrepresents as the highest ideals of humanity. Behind such association is the desire to repulse all that is outwardly different. Only the most primitive stage of organization is achieved through antagonism. There the intellect is not the decisive factor, not the will to progress, but an instinctive association against anything external. In this lower stage of evolution solidarity is achieved by means of hostility instead of reconciliation. Thus Nationalism is an instrument created by disorganization, and can serve only disorganization. The one-sided emphasis of Nationalism creates that very oppression of the nation which it is supposed to remove. Only by the political organization of all mankind can each nation attain its full freedom and become an active agent of human progress. Imperialism, founded on Nationalism, obstructs such free development of the nation. Its fundamental principles of oppression and violent annexation are inherently opposed to national equality and to national greatness. Here again it proves to be the great obstacle in the way of natural evolution.

Imperialism does not change the final

course of world-history, but for a time it does distort and mislead human thought. It prevents the recognition of natural tendencies, and forces humanity with infinite toil and suffering to fight its way back from the side-paths into which it had been misled, on to the highroad of true social progress. It destroys the life of generations. With tremendous industry its apostles seek to give it a scientific political basis. The great teachings of Darwin, which promised such a wonderful insight into the secret processes of nature, have been distorted by the Imperialists and misapplied to politics. In transferring the doctrine of the Struggle for Existence of the various species to the entirely different struggle of social organizations within a species, they made a *fatal error*. Novicow,[1] who was the first to refute these misconceptions, has shown that struggle, which is universal among stars, animals, plants and men, follows different methods in each case.

[1] Novicow's thought has recently been made available in English in George Nasmyth's "Social Progress and the Darwinian Theory" (Putnams, 1916).

The stars attract matter; the stronger animal eats the weaker, and by digestion transforms it into a part of its own self. But one celestial body cannot chew another, nor can a lion attract cells away from an antelope. The astronomic struggle is different from the biological, and so is the sociological. The fact that the lion tears open the antelope does not imply that the massacre of the population of one state by that of another is a natural law. But Imperialism leads us into just such a sea of error. It breeds racial conceit and turns a noble patriotism into Chauvinism.

The insanest product of Imperialism is *the system of competitive armament* which has characterized the last generation. Here again an institution quite justifiable in itself has been transformed and caricatured. There can be no rational objection if a group of men seek to protect their peculiar institutions by measures which enable them to repel attacks from without. Even when the world-state is completely organized, some form of military force may still be necessary, just as the police persist in the individual states and cities. The irrationality of the present system consists in the fact that Imperialism has made an instrument intended for defence into a means of realizing Imperialist ambitions of aggression and subjugation. This altered purpose makes armaments relative and always incomplete because their true purpose is never defined. They have ceased to be merely defensive. They have become a means for attaining certain Imperialist ends. Thus military safety is no longer dependent upon the attainment of a certain absolute strength, determined by the defensive needs of the state, but on the *relation* of one state's armament to that of others. The value of armament came to depend solely upon *its permanent superiority to that of other nations*. An uninterrupted increase of armament became imperative in the endless pursuit of that unattainable Utopia. It was an attempt to square a circle. The reciprocal increase permitted no pause, but became faster and madder every day. For it is inherent in the system of armament that the protection which it gives a state is greater the more that state menaces other states. So long as international anarchy persists, armament protects only so long as it menaces, and the tendency of Imperialism is to accentuate its menacing character. But since this menace forces other states to increase their measures of protection, the whole system of competitive armament came to resemble a great juggernaut which in its course destroys the whole civilization of the nations which are seeking national "security." The self-contradiction of international anarchy could not be shown more clearly than by this unreasonable system of competitive armament. In contrast to organization — the natural system of conservation of energy — it is the unnatural high-water mark of wasted energy.

Nevertheless, here as everywhere, the natural tendency to association, the will to reason in the midst of madness, can be discovered in the attempt to attain some permanency despite the increasing friction and the threatening conflicts. The tremendous expenditure on armament made it possible to overcome some of the frictions caused by world-commerce, simply by causing fear that these huge instruments might be used. Thus they actually worked for the peaceful settlement of difficulties — a result which might have been attained by organization with less effort and more certainty.

But in still another fashion the armament system shows the influence of the tendency to interdependence. Imperialism, in seeking world-domination, saw the possibility of a world of united enemies. Competitive armament offered no relief for such a predicament. A state may be convinced that it can become stronger than one other, or than a group of other states, but even this insanity could not deceive it into believing that it could be stronger than all the others put together. So they sought a partial form of association through alliances, — partly to strengthen themselves, partly with the hidden purpose of reducing the power of their opponents by limiting their possibilities of alliance. Those were the first faltering baby-steps towards international organization. But they suffered from the fact that they were made unconsciously, without a full recognition of cause and purpose, experimentally and in the dark, under mechanical compulsion. Thus it happened that in recent years governments sometimes justified their increases of armaments by the necessity of *fulfilling obligations to their allies*. A dim suspicion that association was the way out of anarchy seemed to prevail, but the courage to take the decisive step was lacking. They stopped half way, and that half-work is taking its revenge to-day. The system of alliances which might have been so noble a beginning, led to the world-catastrophe.

But is not even this world-war a proof of the existence of a tendency to interdependence? It was not the system of alliances alone that allowed a local dispute to grow into a conflict of all the great powers of

Europe. It was that community of interests which makes all the nations fellow-sufferers in every war on the surface of the earth. Bound by commerce and trade, they are also fellows in the convulsions of international anarchy. Not only the warring nations, but the so-called neutrals as well, are fellow-fighters, if without direct use of arms; in any case they are fellow-sufferers. This local conflict grown into a world-war must prove to the blindest what a stage of world-organization has already been attained. Misery and sorrow, death and destruction, have spread over every part of the earth, just because the normal course of life was upset at one point. The cry uttered at the beginning of the Austro-Serbian conflict in 1909, "Localize the conflict," is a telling witness of the non-recognition of the change which had come over political relationships. The conflict could not be localized. The only alternative to a peaceful settlement was a European war, a world-catastrophe. And the fact that laborers in Chicago, Rio de Janeiro and South

Australia are unemployed and suffering to-day,[1] is proof that the Serbian idea of national expansion was more important to them and less remote than they had imagined. The world-war is thus a new proof of the interdependence of humanity and a demonstration of the foolishness of the methods of the past. Even in this dark cup there is a gleam of light.

Such glints of light give some comfort. They indicate how blindly mankind is driven, how little we control the course of evolution. As long as men are deceived by such false teachings as Imperialism, they will continue to play this unworthy rôle. Not until we open our eyes and cast aside these errors, will humanity tread the path of progress with the imperishable genius of its kind.

We have recognized international anarchy as the result of the maladaptation of political institutions to the natural tendency of human groups to become interdependent.

[1] Written early in 1915. — Tr.

Imperialism is the false instrument by which men, trusting to the experiences of a previous period of history, have sought to remedy this situation. Consequently, instead of coöperating by mutual agreement, they have had recourse to brute force, and have been driven into that mad rivalry in armament which led to this world-war.

Imperialism still prevails, but its sway is no longer undisputed. One group has recognized the direction of evolution, has seen the evil of international anarchy and analyzed its causes, and has pointed out by what means this greatest evil of humanity can be done away with. *Pacifism* has arisen to oppose Imperialism; it is gaining ground and has begun to use its influence to adapt the political relations of states to their natural tendencies. The system of force still dominates, but it has met worthy opposition. Pacifism has not been without influence. The catastrophe does not prove that pacifism was wrong, but that it was not sufficiently influential. The war, demonstrating as it does the failure of

Imperialism, will undoubtedly increase the prestige of pacifism.

Pacifism had already stirred the will to international organization. It had already created institutions to serve this organization. A tremendous campaign was in progress the world over. The contest between the supporters of the old philosophy of force and the new school of thought was uninterrupted. Step by step the apostles of force and the believers in anarchy were driven back. They fought with the lowest weapons of calumny, insult and scorn. They could not refute the pacifist position, so they tried to discredit it. Such methods cannot bring permanent success. The principles of pacifism spread.

The institutions of the Hague, so laughed at by the militarists, — just as robber knights once scoffed at the "Truce of God," — are a valuable and visible sign of pacifist progress. True, to-day, amid the thunder of cannons, he who makes merry over the empty Palace of Peace by the sand-dunes of Scheveningen, is sure of the applause of the mob. But jests cannot destroy such a work. The Mausers, the submarines and the dreadnoughts plying their trade in the neighborhood of the Palace of Peace seem more important to-day, but they are not!

The Hague Palace and the instruments of destruction are products of the same human genius, but the latter are products of human misunderstanding, the former of a logical recognition of things as they are. The one serves destruction, the other conservation and construction. It is easy to explain why the cannon and torpedoes are more effective to-day. They are ready for use, and the will to use them is behind them. The work of the Hague is not yet complete; the will to use it does not yet prevail. But it requires only that mankind shall so will, and the machinery of the Hague will function as effectively as do the marvels of military technique to-day, and these in turn will be as dumb and powerless as is now the Palace on the coast of Holland. The tool can never complete the deed without the human will behind it. To-day that will is behind the tools of militarism. But the battle is on to put that will behind the instruments of law and order.

The Hague Conventions are one product of this battle. They are a compromise between the old and the new. The representatives of the old could not prevent their being made — they were compelled to agree to that; but they prevented their receiving binding force. The Hague treaties are voluntary rather than compulsory, recommendations rather than obligations, more apparent than real. In so far the believers in force triumphed. To-day they laugh scornfully because those Conventions have broken down. Their attitude shows the character of the opposition which pacifism has to meet. They who were themselves the cause of that weakness, now seek to prove by that weakness the untenability of pacifism. That is not fighting fairly.

None knew better than the pacifists what was to be expected from those agreements.

We fully realized they could not always prevent war. We regarded them rather as a moral achievement. In this compromise with the believers in force, we saw only the first victory of our point of view over that of lawlessness. We knew that so long as there was no international organization, war, which we regarded as an explosion of force, — whether spontaneous or deliberate, — could not be prevented by rational measures, because the conflict was fundamentally irrational. We knew that in the chaotic conditions of international life, rational methods of settlement would have no chance if the slightest cloak of legal justification could be thrown over the use of force — as it almost always can be. Since such decorative and modest cloaks of legality have nothing whatever to do with the essential conflicts, legal institutions could, under the circumstances, have no importance. Only when the nations did not want war, because the dispute seemed too unimportant, or because the general situation was unfavorable, did they avail themselves of the institutions which pacifism had created. The immediate causes of the present war obviously could have been settled by legal means if all the participants had wished it. But, as we saw in the first chapter, those immediate causes were merely the superficial occasion of the war; the war in reality was the final stage in a long series of conflicts of interest caused by international anarchy. Such conflicts cannot be settled by Hague Conventions.

This, however, does not prove the Hague Conventions superfluous. It only proves that such conflicts cannot be abolished by a mere recommendation to use other means of settlement. Just as force is the product of anarchy, so law is the product of organization. If the conflicts are to be settled by law instead of by war, their character must be modified. When international law takes the place of international lawlessness, international conflicts will lose their menacing character, and will be settled by law. That is where the task of pacifism begins. When this fundamental change in international relations has taken place, the work at the Hague will bear fruit. Then the will of man, the will to establish the reign of law, will animate those technical agreements, and give them life. Then their great importance will be appreciated. To wrest them from the fanatics of force was the first great victory. Let them laugh at the empty Palace of Peace! They hate that building and the treaties behind it. It cannot put the cannon to sleep, but its very existence is a crying protest against the work of cannons — a protest that will yet awaken mankind and destroy the foundations of the whole system of force. From that quiet building there goes forth a warning that will become dangerous to anarchy and its defenders.

The achievements of the Hague are not the only comforting evidence that the sway of militaristic Imperialism is no longer unopposed. I have emphasized them only because they are the most visible sign of the opposing forces of pacifism, and the most immediate means of avoiding the resort to force. Civilization on the eve of war was far more closely knit than most of us realized. Imperialism, the child of anarchy, was still the stronger force, but the evolution toward community of interest and action had made vast progress. The war has produced an attitude of mind which has made it customary to speak of international treaties and international coöperation with scornful superiority, and to consider effort spent on them a waste of energy. Such a point of view is not to be taken seriously; it will disappear after the war as the snow wastes under the spring sun. For these things are no longer mere ideas or Utopian efforts; they are hard facts.

To-day, in the midst of a war which has broken all bonds, there are some who laugh at *international treaties.* Yet it would be hard to imagine a world without treaties. After all, it is a treaty for which this war is being fought, and all the bloody sacrifice is for its sake. When the fever is past, there will surely be a new and higher appreciation of the value of treaties; and the work of international coöperation, interrupted on the 28th of July, 1914, will be resumed. We shall realize that only the inadequate strength of the treaties, and the insufficient recognition of their value to humanity, precipitated the catastrophe. Perhaps we shall remember that it was the infraction of the Treaty of Berlin by one of the parties to it acting without the consent of the others, that brought on the whole miserable business, after that treaty had for a generation protected Europe from its most serious sources of danger.

Internationalism long ago ceased to be a mere idea. It had already exercised an appreciable influence on the life of nations, and established important precedents which gave ground for hope that the nations would adapt their political relations to the natural evolution toward a World-State. An international organization cannot be created, as are other political bodies, by a single deed of force. It must come gradually. The development of international coöperation

INTERNATIONAL ANARCHY 51

demonstrates the progress which had already been made. In other works [1] I have shown how that evolution was progressing in spite of the opposition of the governments. New interests gave a new meaning to old treaties. Common interests became more important than individual. Bipartite treaties were replaced by general agreements, and these dealt less with political matters than with the regulation of general commerce and transportation. The number of international treaties sanctioning violent aggression steadily decreased, while those which provided by general agreement for the peaceful conquest of markets and avenues of trade became more and more frequent. Finally treaties were signed which, instead of merely regulating the conditions existing after a war, were actually intended to prevent war. That was the case at both Hague Conferences, in 1899 and in 1907. Gradually an actual international administration was developed, and the necessary machin-

[1] See, among others, "Handbuch der Friedensbewegung," 2d edition, vol. 1, pp. 118 *sqq*.

ery provided for. Between 1874 and 1909 no less than eighty-six such international agreements were made. The increasing number and importance of the international conferences is an eloquent witness to the development of international organization. From the Congress of Vienna (1815) to 1910 one hundred and fifty-eight such conferences were held. Ten of these came in the first half of the last century, ninety-nine in the second half, and in the first ten years of the present century, there were forty-nine. The demand for organization cannot be more eloquently demonstrated. Formerly such conferences devoted themselves solely to the settlement of the aftermath of war (so the great Congresses of Münster, Utrecht and Vienna); but since the Congress of Vienna only two of these conferences (Paris 1856 and Berlin 1878) have been concerned with past wars, while all the others have had to do with the international regulation of economic, scientific and social affairs. Their character is indicative of the tendency to international organization.

These facts have not been without influence on politics. Treaties became more and more the backbone and scaffolding of the society of nations that was coming into being. The world-war has rather affirmed than disproved this. Were it not that the forces of international anarchy still held the upper hand, this scaffolding would have become stronger and stronger until eventually it was unshakable. But the forces were uneven. The leading spirits did not yet understand the new phenomena and the new necessities. Militaristic ideas triumphed; the forces of anarchy were still in the ascendency. So, quite logically, the world came to that disaster which today appalls us. This must be the high-water mark of anarchy. A change in international relations has become an imperative necessity.

Humanity has before itself the task of shaping a future worthier of itself. Such hopes have been awakened by this war. We begin to see how it has destroyed old prejudices and laid bare old errors, how drastically it has exposed false conclusions and taught new lessons.

CHAPTER III

THE WAR'S LESSONS UP TO DATE

As I write, the war is still in progress. When it is ended, the military strategists will, as after every previous war, study it and prepare to use its lessons for future wars. It is a doubtful undertaking at best, for there is no sphere of human activity so subject to revolutionary technical changes as warfare, and the experience of the present is worth little for the future. Because of the rapid evolution of military technique we can, with General von der Goltz, call the battle of the future the riddle of the Sphinx. Every war teaches new technical lessons. But there are other points of view from which war is just as significant. As a social phenomenon it is of such tremendous importance that its investigation must not be left to military men, who in reality are only interested in its actual conduct.

It must be studied from a sociological viewpoint with the express purpose of discovering *how to avoid such catastrophes in the future.* We need not wait until hostilities cease. Not even then will all the sociological data of the war be at hand. Data will continue to stream in long after the treaty of peace is signed, and some of the most important will come last. The American biologist, David Starr Jordan, rightly emphasized Benjamin Franklin's words, "Wars are not paid for in war-time; the bill comes later." It will be years before all the social effects of this war will be visible. Hence it is our duty to study its lessons while it is still in progress. We cannot postpone its discussion to that distant time when all the material will be available. It is the more important that we fulfil this duty because our purpose is not to wage, but to prevent, future wars. Such a task cannot be begun too soon. In fact, the course of this war, and especially its beginning, offers rich material which can, and indeed must, be evaluated immediately, if our ideas of European restoration are to be realized.

I begin with that problem which the war has proved to be of primary importance — the problem of *armaments*.

In the previous chapter I tried to show that the degeneration of the system of armaments demonstrated the inefficiency of international anarchy. Armaments, although intended for protection, can protect only by menacing others, and these others are forced to adopt counter-measures which in turn menace that state which first sought protection in armament. This reaction led to a competition in armaments which finally became economically intolerable without attaining the security at which it aimed. Armaments have proved themselves deceptive instruments of Imperialism. They give no state a permanent superiority, but merely produce a continuous restlessness and palpitation in all; and such a situation is intolerable in the long run.

Pacifism has consistently pointed out the

fallacy of competitive preparedness, and has emphatically rejected the supposition that it insured peace. Being a symptom of lawlessness, armaments could never secure genuine peace; at most they have lengthened the period between wars and delayed the conversion of "latent" wars into acute, thus maintaining a condition which has nothing in common with that true peace to which we have looked forward. Understanding the causes of this phenomenon, we knew the evil could not be removed by any mere superficial attack, but that its causes must be eliminated — that is, law must be substituted for force. We have often been accused of demanding immediate disarmament, but the serious literature of pacifism contained no such suggestion. "The road to reduction of armaments is by way of international organization. Armaments will disappear of themselves as this organization develops." So I wrote in 1908 in "The Foundations of Revolutionary Pacifism." Positive pacifist effort was directed not against the symptom (armament), but against its causes. Continuous attention to the development of international coöperation, and its conscious furtherance, has always seemed to us the most effective way to eliminate this destructive competition in armaments.

That no other kind of development could bring true peace, that it alone could give security, was clear to us from the beginning. We knew that armament was no peace insurance. In all our writings and at all our congresses we emphasized the fact that armament was not a reliable instrument to maintain even that condition of latent war which most people had become accustomed to call peace. The outbreak of this world-war has shown how foolish was the confidence placed in armaments by the fanatics of force. Their false slogan, "Si vis pacem, para bellum," has proved a hopeless delusion; it was the armaments themselves which finally made war inevitable. We had prepared for war, and our instruments of warfare were so sensitive that they almost fired themselves.

The war has proved what a menace to peace these armaments had come to be.

Pacifist effort was directed to lessening the danger of the conflicts to which international anarchy gave rise, by allowing time for the momentary excitement of the masses and their leaders to die down, thus assuring a calm and rational discussion of the situation. Nothing is more favorable to an explosion of force than the excitement of impending conflict. *Machinery was established providing for dilatory treatment of all severe international disputes*, before they could lead to an open conflict of arms. It was from such considerations that the First Hague Conference created the International Commission of Inquiry, which was further developed at the Second Conference.

The provision referred to, in Article 9 of the "Convention for the pacific settlement of international disputes," reads, "In disputes of an international nature *involving neither honor nor vital interests*, and arising from a difference of opinion on points of fact, the contracting powers deem it expedient and desirable that the parties who have not been able to come to an agreement by means of diplomacy, should, *as far as circumstances allow*, institute an international commission of inquiry, to facilitate a solution of these disputes by elucidating the facts by means of an impartial and conscientious investigation."

It is easy to see how this provision has been qualified and weakened by the traditional spirit of disorganization. It concerns only "disputes involving neither honor nor vital interests." Each state is to define these terms for itself. Even then they dared not recommend the method, but confined themselves to "deeming" it "expedient and desirable," and did not consider its application except "as far as circumstances allow." These limitations are the concessions which the new public mind had to make to the old conceptions of diplomats at the Hague Conferences.

But despite these limitations, the Convention has already had one great success. In the delicate Hull affair, when the departing Russian Baltic fleet fired on English fishing smacks (1904), when the war-spirit on the streets of London rose to fever-heat, a peaceful solution was attained by referring the matter to an International Commission of Inquiry, — simply because the excitement of the moment was thus allayed. There are of course some who will seek to minimize that occasion. Those who take the trouble to go through the daily papers of that time will realize that the dispute, concerning as it did both the "honor and the vital interests" of the participants, was considered very likely to lead to war. It aroused the public more, and seemed more serious, than the dispute which grew into the present war.

The treaties which *Mr. Bryan*, then American Secretary of State, offered to all the countries of the world in 1913 are an extension of this idea of dilatory treatment. Contrary to the general belief, they were not arbitration treaties, but *treaties for the prevention of war*.

The contracting parties pledged themselves to refer any dispute to an international commission of inquiry before going to war. This commission may postpone its report for a year. After it has reported, the states are free to decide whether they will go to war or settle the matter peacefully.[1] But it is quite clear that after a year's delay no dispute will lead to war. That is the fundamental purpose of those treaties. Thirty-four states have assented to them in principle, and at the end of 1914 the United States had signed such treaties with eighteen governments, among them the European countries, Great Britain,

[1] Article I of the Anglo-American treaty reads:

"The High Contracting Parties agree that all disputes between them of every nature whatsoever, to the settlement of which previous arbitration treaties or agreements do not apply in their terms or are not applied in fact, shall, when diplomatic methods of adjustment have failed, be referred for investigation and report to a permanent International Commission, to be constituted in the manner prescribed in the next succeeding article; and they agree not to declare war or to begin hostilities during such investigation and before the report is submitted."

From Article 3:

"The report of the International Commission shall be completed within one year after the date on which it shall declare its investigation to have begun, unless the High Contracting Parties shall limit or extend the time by mutual agreement."

WAR'S LESSONS UP TO DATE 63

France, Spain, Switzerland, Denmark and Holland.

There can be no doubt that dilatory treatment of this sort could have settled the dispute which led to this war, had use been made of the machinery of the Hague Conventions established for that very purpose. But the provision of the Hague Conference in regard to a Commission of Investigation has remained a scrap of paper for the same reason which was responsible for the failure of the Hague Conventions in general — because the machinery was not supported by the will to use it. There was one other reason, to which I referred on page 23. *The apparatus of armament had become so tremendously sensitive* that, although created to preserve peace, it was so perfectly prepared for war that when a dispute reached its climax, a postponement even of a few hours was impossible. A few days' delay, even twenty-four hours' delay, would give the enemy an advantage that might never have been regained. That is why Austria-Hungary refused to extend the time allowed Serbia to answer her ultimatum, refused to take part in the Conference of Ambassadors proposed by Sir Edward Grey, and did not respond to the Serbian proposal to refer the dispute to the Hague; and that is why Germany refused the similar proposal made by the Czar on the twenty-ninth of July, and allowed Russia but twelve hours to answer her ultimatum. Russia had begun to mobilize, and every German decision was dominated by the fear that if the Czar's proposals for pacific settlement were accepted, Russia would get the start and have the military advantage. This delicately balanced system of armament, this extreme "preparation for peace," actually led to war.

Thus experience has confirmed our contentions that armament alone does not insure peace, and furthermore that the constant increase of armament is an actual menace to peace. Armament makes all the machinery created to secure peace a mere illusion. In contrast to the pacifist method of securing peace by delay, the anarchical method of "insuring" peace by increasing armament makes rapid action imperative.

The over-sensitive system of armament was not the sole cause of the war. No small part was played by the hope of anticipating increases planned by the enemies of Germany. The knowledge that the Russian land and sea forces were to be strengthened, and strategic railways built on her western border, and that France was about to reintroduce the three-year compulsory service, weakened opposition to war in Germany and prevented a peaceful settlement. It may have been the expectation of a relatively less favorable position as regards armament, quite apart from such immediate disadvantage as a delay would have brought, which made the responsible military leaders think it inadvisable further to postpone the conflict.

How often has preparedness been praised as the surest guarantee of peace, as a cheap insurance premium against the losses of war!

The outbreak of the present war has proved that these sacrifices of strength and wealth were made to an illusion, that *the armaments themselves inhibited rational means of adjustment;* indeed, that the system of competitive armament inseparable from preparedness finally left no way out but war — to avoid which the whole system was supposedly established!

How can the expenditure of more such billions be justified when it is evident that all this preparation not only was unable to prevent this most fearful of all wars, but actually caused it? It can no longer be said that it was armament that kept Germany at peace forty-four years. It is a not a question of armament alone but of *competition* in armament. It did indeed postpone open war, but it only postponed it, and never for a single hour did it give us any real security. All through these four and forty years there has been the constant danger of war. We have never enjoyed true peace; only the sparse fruits of a very dangerous truce have been ours. No reasonable person will demand that we disarm and stand defenceless. But we must learn the grave lessons of this war, that a peace secured by big guns is not enough, that means must be found to establish a new system of international relationships not founded on the mere accumulation of instruments of war. That is one of the lessons which this war has already taught us, and it is not the least important.

The world-war has confirmed another important pacifist principle. It has demonstrated the ineffectiveness of attempts to *humanize and regulate warfare*. The pacifist doctrine has always been that force cannot be legalized, and that such a reversion to the primitive as war is incapable of humanization. It is just as impossible to limit the efficiency of instruments of destruction as to prescribe regulations for the manner in which an overheated steam-boiler shall crack. It is an impossible attempt to change the inevitable sequence of cause and effect. As Eucken somewhere says, men sometimes wish the stones of their buildings to be soft, if they happen to fall on their heads. War suspends all the laws of morality, it sets aside the laws of society, and restores the primitive condition of unrestricted lawlessness. At such a time there cannot be order. *A condition of anarchy may be completely done away with, but it cannot be regulated.* Many, not pacifists, who think that war is still indispensable, admit this. Again and again military men have told us that the greatest inhumanity in war is the greatest humanity, because it exhausts the enemy most quickly, thus hastening peace and avoiding much sacrifice and misery. "There is no such thing as humane warfare. The purpose of every war is the physical destruction of the enemy." So said Dr. Dernburg, formerly Colonial Secretary, to a voter who asked him for material to refute certain accusations in connection with the war in Southwest Africa.

It cannot be denied that some forbearance in war is both possible and necessary, and that protection of the prisoners and wounded

WAR'S LESSONS UP TO DATE

has saved many lives. But it is not always possible, nor can we expect that the existing rules will be obeyed without exception. Even in time of peace it is impossible to keep the brute instincts of some individuals within the bounds of law; how much less is it possible in time of war, when such people can give their instincts free rein! We do not want to abolish the Red Cross; but we must not expect too much of it, nor content ourselves with it alone. True humanity consists in protecting human life and health from the dangers of war, not in making the consequences of those dangers more tolerable. Such endeavors are never more than a makeshift. They save some, but they cannot prevent others from perishing without help or care; many wounded men and prisoners are killed by the hardships of the system.

This is true of all the various attempts to regulate warfare. The sufferings of the civil population, the destruction of public buildings and works of art, of private estates, the sinking of ships and their passengers, the use of hunger and fire as weapons, — all these which those who sought to humanize warfare had come to regard as things of the past, have, despite all the well-meant attempts to prevent them, been horribly common in this war. Such atrocities do not demonstrate unlimited cruelty inherent in human nature, but rather the simple impossibility of proceeding otherwise with instruments fashioned for that very purpose, instruments which cannot but be cruel.

There are a number of reasons why atrocities beyond comprehension are more frequent in this than in previous wars. War was never before fought on so huge a scale, with such masses of men, or with such perfected weapons. The destruction has inevitably been greater and more permanent. If the best heads in the world occupy themselves for decades in devising the quickest and most effective means for destroying human life, human institutions and human property, something very perfect in the way of destruction is bound to follow. This war is not qualitatively more inhumane than previous wars; but *quantitatively its cruelty surpasses them all* and therefore it horrifies us. Furthermore, war was never before waged in such civilized regions. To the amount of destruction caused by the extension of the theatre of war and the effectiveness of its instruments is added the fact that the men opposing each other are very highly civilized and the region very highly cultivated. Never before was war waged so publicly. It makes a difference whether war be waged in Manchuria or Thrace, or in the very centre of European civilization. Europe is closer to us, both in space and in feeling, and the desperate cries of its inhabitants are listened to and comprehended as those from the remote parts of the earth which have suffered from war in recent years, were not. No, no! War as such is not more cruel than in the past, but we are more affected by it because we ourselves have become more sensitive.

If the ancient civilization of the peoples now at war is unable to modify the horrors and sufferings of the machine-made war of to-day, if the modern European cannot escape the compulsion to cruelty inherent in war, what success can we expect from these various rules and regulations in the future? It is all very well for carefully educated, well-clothed, highly moral gentlemen, sitting around a green table under the protection of the law, to discuss them. Safe in port it is easy to make regulations for the conduct of passengers in case of shipwreck. But we are not horrified if the affrighted crowd, in the moment of danger, when the ship is sinking, does not obey the rules. We explain the panic psychologically. And in time of war — an infinitely greater catastrophe — can we expect the conscientious observance of rules made in time of peace? That would be to misunderstand human nature and the nature of war, whose express purpose it is to disregard the dictates of humanity.

The men who codified the laws of war had more psychological insight than those in various countries who wax angry over their violation. Any one reading with care the provisions of the Hague Conventions with regard to the laws of warfare on land and sea will observe that they were written less in the hope that they would really be obeyed than as a rather becoming decoration for our civilization. In no other way can those clauses be understood which retract in one paragraph what was said in the preceding; those clauses which read "as far as is compatible with military necessity," "under certain circumstances," "as far as is possible," etc. They disclose how well the authors were aware that practice would play havoc with their theory. They added those limitations only to save their own souls.

The discussion at the Hague shows how conscious they were of the self-contradiction of the attempt to regulate warfare. In replying to the American plea for the immunity of private property at sea one of the delegates, the representative of a small maritime country, said that the possibility of destroying commerce in time of war was one element in the defence of small nations. It had been called a relic of piracy: "That is true, just as it is true that war is nothing but organized murder. We retain this right only for the time when normal life has ceased. We simply cannot tie our hands at the very moment when justice disappears to be replaced by force, when pity veils its eyes and inexorable brute force is supreme." That was an honorable admission which lacked nothing in logic. At a time when by common consent force dominates, when everything depends upon force, regulations and restrictions cannot expect to be observed. They are mere decoration. Mankind, conscious that war is an unworthy institution incompatible with the demands of an enlightened age, has by such provisions for regulation and humanization only sought to deceive its awakening conscience. *These provisions are merely the fig-leaf which mankind demands after eating of the tree of knowledge.* No more than a fig-leaf can cover the nakedness of the body, can any number of Geneva and Hague Conferences humanize warfare.

Only the war could prove this. The lesson is of great importance. It will sharpen the sense of responsibility among those in power, and strengthen the *demand for peace* among the masses. War is a bestial institution, and he who would protect mankind from its evils must do more than attempt to regulate it; he must work for its abolition.

All else is humbug!

We must refuse to listen to those who say that the war has shown that international law is bankrupt. They err. *International law has not failed, but merely the so-called laws of war*, which were never truly law at all. For war is the cessation of law. True international law is that law which human society has developed for its normal activity; it rests upon the foundations of our civilization; it has been created by reason for the promotion of organization. Only fools would give up such order for unfettered force, or would establish a kind of law which, self-contradictory as it would be, would inevitably fail at the firing of the first shot.

Another thing this war has taught us is a clear recognition of the changed function of *war as a political instrument*. Many, judging from the European wars of the past, had been quite misled. There were still many people who thought of war as a short but rejuvenating letting of blood, disturbing the peaceful course of human events for a time, but promising an acceleration of progress in the future. *The catch-phrase of a "fresh and merry" (frisch und fröhlich) war is at last dead forever*, and with it have gone all the beauty and romance of war.

It is unfortunate that experimental proof was required to rid us of so outgrown a conception. The arithmetical proposition ought to have been enough. But we were too deep set in tradition and we did not want to get away from it. We have learned only a little of the real cost of this war, but there are enough data already at hand to convert those who still maintain so petty a conception of war and seek to deceive the people with it. The magic of military romance is gone forever. The mountains of corpses, the legions of cripples, the one-armed, the one-legged, blind, infected, consumptive, those afflicted with heart diseases and the insane, and the smoking ruins already left behind by the war, the property destroyed, the capital and savings lost, and, not least, the bleeding hearts and shattered nerves, make such a mass of misery and despair that not even the most expert whitewashers will ever again be able to conceal the facts.

We were deceived. We believed that that which we call war to-day was the same as that which was called by the same name in days gone by, simply because it was unchained in the same old way. Modern war is as incomparable to the knightly expeditions of past centuries as the explosion of a match to an eruption of Vesuvius. The instrument which man once controlled has grown beyond his control. He is no longer master, but is servant of a thing which, once set free, he cannot master. Clausewitz' definition of war as a continuation of politics, "but with different instruments," is no longer applicable. The instruments are too expensive. *War can no longer be described as a continuation of politics; it is an open admission of the bankruptcy of politics.*

This will be impressively evident when we come to view the present catastrophe as a whole. The things that will come to light will tell such a tale that the glorifiers of war will hardly dare again to ply their dangerous trade; and if they do, their voices will be overwhelmed by the terrible burden of facts. They will hardly succeed in making new converts. Militarism has been dealt a blow from which it can never recover. The apostles of force will be silenced.

The dream of romantic war is ended. The human earthquake of 1914 led to a fearful awakening.

The *technical* lessons of the war are also important. Sorrowfully we pacifists noted with what surprise the new forms of war were greeted. Half a generation ago *Jean Bloch,* one of our own movement, predicted most of these phenomena almost exactly as they are happening to-day, with only such differences as can be accounted for by the further technical development of arms and transportation.

Jean Bloch appeared before the public in the late nineties with his big six-volume book on war, in which he sought to prove that the revolution in military technique, and the economic and social evolution of Europe, had caused such changes that it was doubtful whether a war between the equally armed great powers of Europe would ever lead to any result.

He showed that the rapid evolution of military technique made the experience of past wars useless, and that the revolutionary changes in munitions required a new science of tactics. The necessity of fortified trenches, transforming war into a prolonged siege, the superiority of the defence, the huge losses, the long duration of the battles, their indecisiveness for the course of a campaign, and the unprecedented shock to economic life caused by the extraordinary length of the war, — all these Bloch described in detail. He called attention to the vast extension of the battlefields, to the resultant difficulties in the commissary, to the insufficient provision for the wounded. He referred to the tremendous sacrifice of these huge battles, and described the future war as so sinister a thing that he doubted whether the nerves of civilized Europeans could bear the shock. From these premises he concluded — we cannot yet verify his results — that the gigantic catastrophe of a modern war would be so bloody and destructive and the combatants would emerge from it so weakened that there would be no real victors or vanquished, and only the complete physical and economic exhaustion of the combatants would perforce put an end to hostilities.

Bloch was certainly mistaken in many respects, especially as regards the supposed impossibility of prolonged toleration of economic disturbance. In respect to armaments and economic developments there was much that he, at the end of the past century, could not foresee. *But he was right in the essentials;* the present war has vindicated his teachings. Whether the war will end as he predicted, only the future can tell. It almost looks as if he were right. The war has already taught us that states such as the great powers of Europe, or allied groups of such states, cannot be forced to their knees according to the old recipe. This war will not end with a victorious conqueror dictating terms of peace to a vanquished opponent, as all the belligerents at first expected. We have much to unlearn. In modern war there are no impetuous charges; there are no hills whence the general, seated astride a fiery charger, surveys the battle through a field glass. The pictures of our schooldays are no longer true to life; and the end will be as different from the stories. The immensity of the states at war entirely excludes the possibility of complete defeat. There will have to be a compromise in the end — and one which could have been made much more cheaply before the war began.

Bloch's intention was to make this chain of reasoning clear. He had no desire to stand in history as a soothsayer and prophet; he wished to be a monitor and to teach a method of international settlement different from the old, which seemed to him so ineffective. His doctrine was not built on any new discoveries; he had simply collected the works of military authorities; but he drew conclusions from them as a sociologist instead of as a strategist. He was little appreciated by his contemporaries. The Hague Conferences were said to have been called as a result of his book, but he was unable to influence their negotiations as he desired. As an outsider he lectured in the evenings to the Hague delegates. In vain he called upon the governments not to believe or disbelieve him blindly, but to test his conclusions. In vain! They preferred to be surprised fifteen years later by events which they might have learned from him to foresee.

This war may bring recognition to our prophet, for it is proving in practice the truth of his theory. Europe has undertaken a bloody investigation. *Perhaps this pacifist, so little understood by his own contemporaries, will emerge the only victor in the war.* Perhaps then a Europe, grown wiser by its wounds, will commemorate him by a bronze statue on one of its highest peaks.

In the preceding chapter I spoke of some of the other lessons which the war has taught us. That the world has already become an economic unit, which if disturbed at one point, suffers in all parts of the organism; that the political interrelationships were already so highly developed that — at least in Europe — wars could no longer be "localized"; that war in any case, wheresoever and by whomsoever it might be waged, is, since all suffer by it, a serious matter for every nation on earth — these things the history of the last few months has taught us. There is no need further to discuss them. At the conclusion of the hard struggle there will be still other and decisive lessons to be learned.

When the war began we heard much of the need to unlearn and to relearn (*umlernen*).

We must indeed learn anew, but not in the sense in which the phrase was first used. We must at last accustom ourselves to the fact that war is no longer to be regarded as a useful instrument of human evolution, but as its most dangerous impediment, which, whatever else may happen, must be eliminated.

CHAPTER IV

THE TREATY OF PEACE AND FUTURE PEACE

"Every war ends in peace." —

That is another of those aphorisms which are repeated parrotlike when they no longer contain an atom of truth. We have known for centuries that the earth moves around the sun; nevertheless we still speak in mediæval terms of the "rising" and the "setting" of the sun. Just as old and just as untrue is the saying that war ends in peace; but there is this difference, that the fundamental untruth of the latter phrase is not so generally understood as of that which Galileo exposed. It is a very dangerous phrase. Wars have never ended in true peace. They usually end with a treaty of peace that stops armed hostilities and introduces a condition of latent hostility, but which leaves the community of nations in just as primitive a condition as before.

The disorganization and national isolation persist; when a treaty of peace is signed with the usual courtesies, acute war is merely transformed into latent. As I have pointed out, that condition may have been quite tolerable when each state was self-sufficient, before the natural tendency to interdependence had made itself felt. But to follow the same old course to-day would be madness, and would mean destruction for the entire European organism. This is not a war which can be ended with a simple treaty of peace. That which we call war is only the final act of a drama which has been convulsing Europe for a generation. It did not begin on the 28th of July, 1914; it began decades ago. To-day it is disclosing the danger in which we have been living; it has created intolerable conditions which are quite incompatible with the evolution of the society of nations. The petty methods of the past are incompetent to overcome this state of things.

It will not do to sign a treaty of peace which does nothing but stop the flow of blood

THE TREATY OF PEACE

and end the most obvious evils of anarchy, leaving everything otherwise as it was before. The task before us is to close a fearful period of human history. It can only be accomplished by *establishing a durable peace*, a true peace, which shall transform international intercourse and set international relations on a new and better track. When, after all these sacrifices, we have at last recognized international anarchy for what it really is, we shall not allow the menace to continue. That perilous catchword according to which this bath of blood would automatically lead to peace, must be cast aside. However painstakingly a treaty be made, if it provides merely for altered boundary-lines and for indemnities, it is insufficient. It would not achieve that true peace at which we aim, and which humanity *must* have.

Instinctively the people and the governments divine the real issue. A certain unanimity of purpose in the midst of the great conflict is clear. It is fearful to realize that all *the people who are fighting so bloodily are fighting for the same end.* They are all fighting, according to their own statements, for their right to existence and their future safety. That end, however, can only be attained by organization. Neither subjugation nor the complete victory of one party over the other will ever bring peace and security to this tormented continent.

Nevertheless each of the warring countries hopes to achieve its purpose in this impossible manner, and refuses to recognize the actual conditions of communal life. Each seeks to establish its own peace and its own security, whereas a genuine peace is possible only by common agreement, by the establishment of harmony; and national security is possible only when there is international coöperation.

Like the pursuer of fortune in the fairy-tale, the nations chase the will-o'-the-wisp of *durable peace*, and each hopes to win it for itself by force of arms and subjugation. The watchword "durable peace" is a promise of salvation to hundreds of millions on the continent of Europe to-day; but there are very few who clearly understand how it may be realized. Most of us have a simple hope that it can be attained by another of those "treaties of peace" such as we have had in the past, which have never yet laid the foundations of permanent peace but always contain the germs of the next war. We think to measure the permanence of that visionary future order by the amount of destruction and humiliation which we can visit upon our opponents. What blindness! That was the method of the ancient Romans, who, at a time when the world was not yet interdependent, sought to extend peace as far as their weapons could strike. That peace came to an ignominious end when other peoples discovered its secret and appeared on the scene with weapons just as strong. In an era of interdependence, when the states are forced to live together, these methods have become inadequate, in proportion as the world is smaller and weapons more effective. *There is no such thing as a durable peace maintained by force, just as there can no longer be peace for one nation apart from the rest (Solofriede); there can be only one peace for all the nations, established upon justice to all.*

This is all so clear and simple that we are horrified at the illusion under which all the warring nations labor. There is a mutual desire to subjugate because there has been a mutual threat. Success is expected from the most perverted methods. They aim to seize as much as possible of the enemy's land, and to weaken him economically; and on such a wavering foundation they all hope to build a permanent peace. They have learned that it is no longer possible to annihilate an enemy or to extirpate a nation of many million inhabitants; but not one of them draws the right conclusion. They do not suspect that the consequence of the use of force for subjugation is rebellion by force; that to-day the most fearfully oppressed nation never gives up the struggle, and that every use of force is therefore an element of disturbance, stimulating intrigue and revenge, and makes nothing less likely than peace and

THE TREATY OF PEACE 91

security. Force brings with it discord, hate and revolt. He who sows force, reaps war.

Shall the old game begin again? Shall the nations be tormented anew by the revengeful passions of oppressed and conquered peoples? Shall the game of armaments be renewed, and on a previously undreamt of scale? Shall all the achievements of human labor and intelligence, all the goods which were to bring happiness and comfort to mankind, be sacrificed to make more and more fearful and destructive weapons in a new and more angry competition of armaments? Shall the tension be so increased that the danger of explosion will be present every hour, so that Europeans will go to bed with the daily thought that the bloody business may recommence the next morning? Can we realize in what a panic humanity will live if the old system persists — more acute and threatening than ever before? Who will feel any stimulus to earn, to save, to care for the future, when he knows that any hour this fearful drama may recur and must recur? Who but will fear to bring up children, to mould their character and to care for their future, if we have a peace which leaves us as before, in anarchy, but in deeper anarchy?

Such would be the "durable peace" which a single nation might establish by the annexation of territory and the economic exhaustion of the enemy. It would be a world inconceivably full of fear if after this convulsive struggle we should content ourselves with a treaty of peace which was a mere interruption of hostilities and did not lay the foundation of a genuine international organization. If such be the result of this struggle, which, we were told, was inevitable because the previous condition of international anarchy had become intolerable, that condition would by contrast seem a paradise. Everything will be sharper, more deadening and more destructive. Wealth aggregating hundreds of billions will have been destroyed. Heavy tax-burdens will be necessary, and they will hamper recuperation. These, and the limitless hate and the embittered feeling of revenge, will make commercial progress slow and painful, and the production of goods will suffer from a limited consumption. Bleeding wounds will prevent international coöperation and will give rise to suspicions which will make it seem the last word of wisdom to renew and increase the competition in armaments, whose burdens the weakened peoples will be less than ever able to bear. The enormous injuries which private property has suffered in this war, the lawlessness which has befallen the stranger everywhere, the horrors which the civil population has had to endure, will increase the previous insecurity and create a state of permanent panic which finally will limit all progress and make any civilization a doubtful possibility.

There is perhaps one consolation in this desperate prospect. It is so intolerable that it must force men to rebel, to seek some release from the afflictions which would be the logical products of a peace made according to the old models.

There must be a change. This explosion,

which has so clearly exposed the instability of the condition in which we have been living, must lead to a complete transformation of international relations, must achieve a genuine and secure peace. *The world-war must destroy its own source, international anarchy,* and result in international organization, in a rational state-system. That which is filling our lives with sorrow to-day shall mould the world anew, and shall accelerate the process of organization.

There is much to encourage us in this belief. Never before were the horrors of war so universal. Previous wars were waged between two opponents or at most between small groups. The other nations took no part, or were bystanders who actually benefited from them. This war comprehends the whole world — not only the belligerent nations, but the others as well, for they also suffer from it. The interests of all mankind are involved; and the common will of the whole world will awaken to put an end to a system that could bear such fruit. This very catastrophe has shown to what extent the foundations for a community of civilized nations had already been laid. That a relatively unimportant conflict of two states inevitably grew into a world-war is sufficient evidence of the existence of that interdependence which should properly have led to world-organization rather than to world-war. The people, and with them their governments, will realize that wars waged on such a scale can no longer be made a part of their political calculations, and that accordingly another method of settlement will have to be devised. When the bill for this outburst is presented, they will recognize, what they refused to accept on the assurance of the pacifists, that the method of war is no longer competent or serviceable.

How can *genuine peace* and international organization be achieved? It is naturally hard to answer this question when we do not yet know under what conditions the governments of the warring nations will meet to discuss the cessation of hostilities. As I said in the previous chapter, I think it practically impossible that we will have to reckon with a complete victory of one group of powers. There will hardly be a victor in the old sense of the word. The new situation will have to be the product of a compromise. At the most the group of allies which have the more favorable position will be able to win some slight advantages. No one will be in a position to dictate the terms of peace.

The great question is whether the governments will place the interests of the future and the necessity of general security above the immediate advantages to individual nations in the bitter struggle which, when the battlefields are silent, will be waged across the green table. Will those who are convoked to end the war appreciate the significance of their task? The same old diplomats, or at least the same old system of diplomacy as that which was unable to remedy the previous international anarchy or to prevent its explosion in war, will be summoned. There may well be doubt whether the events of the war

THE TREATY OF PEACE 97

have so broadened their vision that they are capable of establishing that redeeming system of international organization which alone can firmly establish lasting peace.

Therefore I think it important to look forward to *two separate conferences*, the first to attend to *the cessation of hostilities* by a so-called "treaty of peace," the second to guarantee a genuine peace for the future by *the foundation of a new European international organization*. The separation should be in time as well as in function. The liquidation of war must precede the establishment of peace, and for various reasons a provisional organization must precede the final.

True peace cannot be established by the old discredited diplomacy of the warring nations. It is essential that the representatives of the neutral nations of Europe and of the United States take part in it. This will hardly be possible in the immediate settlement of the war, as the combatants would object to any interference in a matter which concerns them alone. But in the establishment of the future world-order the nations which were not immediate participants in the war, but were nevertheless affected by it, will have a right to share. Thus in such a second stage of the work of peace there would be a greater chance to effect the reorganization of international relations in a modern spirit.

Furthermore, not until after the war will European public opinion attain its old freedom. It has been limited among the neutrals who have had to be so cautious about their neutrality, as well as among the combatants. If we are in earnest in our endeavor to mould the future, we cannot dispense with our most powerful and effective instrument, public opinion.

It is no less important to remember that not until the war is well past will its real damage be evident and all the data be at hand. Such facts will help us in the reorganization of the future, and we cannot afford to dispense with their assistance. Such a task as the reorganization of the Euro-

THE TREATY OF PEACE 99

pean state-system will require very thorough and therefore long deliberation. Were it to be undertaken when the immediate issues of the war were being settled, it would be dangerously hurried. For the disorder of war to continue and the armies to remain in their positions until the last formula for future organization was found and the last name signed, would create an intolerable situation which inevitably would finally lead to a fatal abbreviation of the discussions.

Despite the separation of the two conferences in function and in time, certain things must be demanded of the former. Its first task is of course to end the war; but it must also pave the way for the second undertaking. It would be small comfort to humanity to postpone the establishment of permanent peace, if at the end of the war a situation should be created which imperilled the success of that second conference. Real statesmanship and wisdom will be required. We can look for some help to the logic of events, an influence which will be more powerful after the war. The settlement should avoid any humiliation of either group, or its economic paralysis or exhaustion, and should lay the foundation for the congress that is to follow. Further, this second conference, which will be composed of both combatants and neutrals, must have the right to abrogate or extend the provisions of the previous treaty. The power of all Europe and America standing behind this conference will be sufficient to secure that. The exercise of this power should not be difficult in view of the moral pressure it can bring to bear and of its purpose of securing the general welfare.

It has been proposed that the task of establishing peace be referred to a *Third Hague Conference* to be called immediately after the treaty of peace is signed. I do not agree. The Hague Conferences include all the nations of the world; to refer the further organization of Europe to all of them would be a mistake. Outside of Europe the United States alone really belongs to the European group. Furthermore, the Hague Conferences have

THE TREATY OF PEACE

always laid their chief emphasis on the regulation of war, and their bond of union has perforce been too weak. Thus they are not well adapted to the function of founding a European system or of securing permanent peace. The new organization that such a system would create would lay the foundation necessary for the Hague tribunals to attain their true value. It is better not to refer this matter to the Hague Conference. We must remember that the organization of Europe will not immediately be completed by the mere treaty of peace. It will be only a beginning, a mere foundation. Its extension will be the unremitting task of decades.

Friends of humanity, turning sadly from a Europe thrilled with bloody hallucinations, are revived by the vision of these things that are to be. The hour will come when their work will begin. And we will continue to hope that it will achieve its purpose, that it will end a tragic period of human history and give birth to a happier.

CHAPTER V

INTERNATIONAL PROBLEMS

SINCE the beginning of the war the thought of millions has turned to the future. The number of pacifists has therefore increased. Many who were formerly inaccessible to the teachings of pacifism have, as a consequence of the dramatic instruction of the war, accepted it. Pleasing as this is, it has certain drawbacks. From these newcomers in our movement an ocean of well-meant but often confusing and misleading plans and advice is poured out upon the public. Inevitably those to whom these ideas are new, who are for the most part ignorant of the accomplishments of the past, and often unaware that for decades a great movement has concerned itself with the development of these very ideas, make the mistakes of beginners and become mere *dilettantes*. Because of the ill-will of our

INTERNATIONAL PROBLEMS 103

opponents and their influence upon the public — completely ignorant of pacifism, anything and everything is accepted and condemned as the product of our teachings. This lowers the credit of scientific pacifism. It is the penalty of popularity. The existing organizations of the movement will have to act as a clearing-house and reject amateurish ideas which really retard the progress of pacifism.

Very much the same ideas which moved people fifty or sixty years ago and made the peace movement appear a sentimental dream, are reëmerging to-day. Suggestions which were long ago cast among the Utopias pretentiously reappear. We hear again the song of the "United States of Europe" which Victor Hugo and Garibaldi used to sing; arbitration courts are recommended as a universal panacea, and to enforce their decrees, the apparently simple recipe of an international police is urged. These well-meaning *dilettantes* lack the fundamental conceptions of pacifism. They do not know the difference between latent war and true peace. They fall into the most grotesque phantasies. They think that it is merely a question of the form of agreement which has led humanity astray. They "surprise" us with model treaties worked out to the smallest detail. They fail to note that it is the will which most governments have lacked — the will to Law, the will to submit to such agreements, and the far-sightedness to see their value. Their primitive point of view makes them miss the salient point. They offer us formulas, thinking that humanity is bleeding because it could not discover the secret of their composition. They do not suspect that formulas are merely unimportant accessories. A beautiful treaty for world-organization could be made in twenty-four hours, if only the will were there to give it life and to enforce it.

It is characteristic of political dilettanteism that it misunderstands the *process of social evolution*. It thinks that social organs, like technical, can be made deductively. It seeks to construct a new form of international community life in the same manner as one builds a machine. Such efforts are vain and Utopian.[1] Only from living embryos can social organisms be developed, cultivated and improved; they cannot deliberately be created out of nothing. The rôle of the social reformer is that of a breeder, not of an inventor. In this we see the dilettanteism of those social carpenters who would attempt to ignore the slow process of evolution and attain at once the final goal which soars before them. Such pacifists are dangerous, for their mistakes strengthen our opponents and cast discredit upon more serious programmes. It is therefore necessary to refer to these well-meant but nevertheless harmful efforts which are now attracting an unusual degree of public attention in connection with the great world-wide movement to safeguard humanity against a return to barbarism.

It is consoling to remember that Utopias

[1] See my "Critique of Social Utopias" in my "Handbuch der Friedensbewegung," 2d edition, vol. 1, p. 117.

never endure, and in the end are always wrecked by their own instability. If, however, we can hasten their end by enlightenment, we avoid an unnecessary waste of energy. So it is with especial satisfaction that we note that immediately after the outbreak of the war, new organizations were founded in various countries under the leadership of experienced peace workers. They have set themselves the task of collecting suggestions for the settlement of the immediate problems into a programme looking toward the further evolution of the natural process of organization. The old centres of the movement have also worked out similar programmes and offered them for general discussion. The demands and programmes of the English Union for Democratic Control, the Dutch Anti-Oorlograad, the Swiss Committee for the Study of the Foundations of a Permanent Treaty of Peace, the Interparliamentary Bureau, the Council of the International Peace Bureau, and various other old and new national organizations in Europe and in America, seeking

INTERNATIONAL PROBLEMS

to serve public opinion with outlines for the discussion of the great world-problems, stand in pleasant relief to the organized and unorganized dilettanteism which is so current.

There are all sorts of problems having to do with the extension of internationalism, which we ought to test and discuss in detail.

It is important that there be no compulsion in this *organization of the nations*. It is illogical to think compulsion necessary, or to believe international coöperation inconceivable without external force. That which was essential in founding the nations need not necessarily have the same importance for the future state-system. Here compulsion becomes an actual hindrance. Coherence in such a system can be maintained by the interest of the parts in the existence of the whole. This interest will of course develop only gradually, but it will grow as the organization grows. The more developed the organism, the greater will be the advantage to the participants, and the greater their interest in its preservation. That is a surer bond than mere compulsion. The greater tenacity of self-interest is clear even in such recent amalgamations as the German and British Empires. Even the experiment tried since 1906 under the influence of the United States and the great republics of South America, of creating a state-system out of the Central American nations, which were formerly continuously at war, seems to be succeeding.

It is a mistake always to look upon the United States of America as a model for Europe. Different historical developments demand different treatment. At most we look forward to an association of the states of Europe, in which self-interest, not compulsion, produces and maintains association. The federations of the past have all rested on compulsion. Either they were formed under the influence of some external force which impelled the states to union, or of one state which, having assumed leadership over a group, compelled the others to join with it. The essential characteristic of the super-state is not the suspension of sovereignty in the individual states, but its utilization in the interests of the whole. My formula for a European state-system therefore would be: "The exchange of individual power for mutual obligations."

The nearest model for Europe is the Pan-American system, which involves a sort of coöperative union (*Zweckverband*) of the twenty-one sovereign American republics. I shall discuss the "Coöperative Union of Europe" in the next chapter. The many plans now emerging for local European economic unions are of this same type. But it would be a mistake to limit a European system to a part of the continent. Inevitably a second would arise, and the disorder, although limited, would not be eliminated. As a transition stage such a local economic union would indeed be an advance; but a further stage of organization is already possible if only we attend to the pressing needs of the time and do not let ourselves be too much influenced by the bitternesses of the moment. Even Europe is too small an area for a serviceable organization. The interests of mankind embrace the whole earth. World organization in the sense referred to is no longer a Utopia; why then should we be content to organize only a part of Europe?

Among the most immediate of the international problems which have to do with this reorganization is *the transformation of European diplomacy.* It has often been pointed out that diplomacy has changed little since the time of Cardinal Richelieu. This is very significant in view of the new tasks which confront it. The outbreak of this war made it clear that diplomacy had become a danger and that its reformation from tip to toe was a necessity. No thinking person will assert that ten or six or perhaps only three persons should decide whether millions are to have their heads cut off or not. A system that maintains such a possibility is not fit for our age. And the fact that there are still diplomats who are willing to accept such a responsibility is sufficient evidence of the untenability of the system. Only the consciousness that no accounts will have to be rendered to the people whose business they manage, or that those accounts will never be audited, can give present-day diplomats the courage to accept such a responsibility. In this age of complete publicity their trade, on which the happiness of generations and empires is so often dependent, is secret. They have no rebuke to fear but that of history; and that will not bother them until this earthly pilgrimage is done. They tell us that it is in the people's interests that diplomatic negotiations be conducted in secret. But the people do not wish that secrecy; they would prefer to resign an advantage which may compel them blindly to risk their lives. The complexity of the modern world makes publicity an indispensable condition, the omission of which is disastrous.

Secrecy is not the only danger of diplomacy. It is dominated by a spirit which would do honor to mediæval chivalry. Any one who reads the diplomatic white papers published at the beginning of the war will observe with disgust this *knightly relic of a vanished age*. In those critical eleven days of European history the lives and happiness of millions were at stake, and the diplomats, coldly smiling, refused to discuss this matter or that, directly or at all. They preferred detours to direct negotiations; they refused peaceful methods of settlement for reasons of etiquette, or with an irrefutable reference to that idol of their cult, Prestige. *The Moloch of the old sagas never devoured so many human beings as this modern idol.* It is the proud achievement of his priesthood that, treating him in their secret negotiations with unprecedented respect, they have made his image seem alive, and have made it an influence in our age of machinery and of world-revolutionizing ideas.

This is not the only idol which is supported and fed with human bodies. There is the antiquated conception of *sovereignty*, to which diplomacy gives an interpretation which long ago ceased to be inherent in it. A state is sovereign over its members, for whom it exercises sovereignty, when it is called upon to act for them. But that does not imply immovability, or a sheer iron inflexibility utterly opposed to the nature of the present-day world, in which no state could exist for an hour without reciprocal limitations and concessions. Modern diplomats use sovereignty as a bulwark behind which they hide when there is no rational justification for their actions.

The diplomats know very well why they wish these idols respected. They find protection behind them, and their work is thus facilitated. We pacifists, who are trying to free humanity from its self-imposed burden, are often accused of playing all around the busy world instead of dealing with plain hard facts. That would be no accusation to the diplomats who control the destinies of Europe to-day. They do not have to bother with realities. If an obstacle they cannot overcome is in their way, they let the people split their skulls about it. For they must guard the idol of "prestige" and the dogma of "sovereignty," and the old conception of war as a continuation of politics, if indeed "with other instruments." They, who are the real Utopians, because they are not compelled to deal with realities, are considered wise heads and "practical politicians" because they use that *pons asinorum* which mankind still calls "other instruments of diplomacy." The desire to end insanity is called Utopianism; to act insanely is statesmanlike wisdom.

The world-war has shown the failure of such statesmanlike wisdom. An institution which can have such consequences can no longer enjoy the confidence of the peoples at whose cost the game is played and lost. It must be changed. We have no need of caste-diplomacy. Only such men as are already eminent in other fields, be it as scholars or as engineers or agriculturists or merchants or teachers, should be called to negotiate between nations. The essential condition for so important an office must no longer be noble blood or high patronage. A committee at least of the national assembly, in critical times the entire national assembly,

INTERNATIONAL PROBLEMS

should coöperate in all negotiations with foreign governments or their representatives. Never again should treaties which have not received parliamentary indorsement be binding.

In some such way the system must be changed. There is nothing in the life of nations more outgrown and more dangerous. Something adapted to our age must replace it.

Closely related to the wretched system of European diplomacy is the *system of alliances* which has grown out of it, which has assisted to maintain international anarchy and has hastened its final collapse. Here again diplomacy has displayed its ignorance of the real conditions of the age. How often have the diplomats, on both sides of the European camp, represented these close alliances as the guardians of European peace! They paid no heed to the course of events by which, so long as international anarchy persisted, every protective measure was transformed into a menace, and national defences were kneaded into huge menacing machines, which in the end left Europe in permanent insecurity and in danger of destruction. In describing the events which led to these alliances, I suggested that a dim suspicion that the salvation of humanity would be found in association, found its half-fulfilment in this system. That incomplete association was in fact a certain protection against hasty wars. The individual state was no longer master of its own decisions, but had to receive the assent of its allies before it could embark upon a war. Since wars affect different states differently, and the consent of the most reluctant must be given, a certain automatic security was achieved. I regarded the allies as natural mediators. Several instances in recent years have corroborated this view. But finally the system failed, and the anarchical character of the alliance system had its way. The incompleteness of that very system of alliances which, consciously and deliberately carried to its logical conclusion, would have given Europe complete security, caused a relatively unimportant conflict to grow into a world-conflagration.

It was the alliance system which gave a new impulse to competition in armament and so enhanced the danger which it originally sought to avoid. But its most dangerous product was an atmosphere of hate and distrust, which cultivated militarism, hindered economic progress, and made life in recent years quite intolerable. There is but one hope left, that the conflagration caused by this dangerous kind of "protection" will destroy it to the last ash. The old system of rival alliances, each seeking only to strengthen itself by the inclusion of other states, will have to end after the war. If the allied states themselves do not end it, then the neutrals, fellow-sufferers in the war, who have had quite sufficient experience of what the Colossus means, will see to it — and their influence after the war will surely not be small — that these menacing alliances cease to play a rôle.

Alliances cannot be ended by a simple decree. It is of no use to forbid them. Even after the war there will be no power strong enough to carry out such a decree. Even within the nations it will be difficult to combat the evil, for only a very powerful state would undertake a parliamentary decree to enter no alliances. The others will refrain from alliances only when to do so has become the general rule; and that will happen only when the method of common action in the work of restoration is so far developed that the nations find in it a real substitute for the poor system of individual alliances. That is not so difficult as it seems. It is only a matter of a second step following the first. The Triple Alliance and the Triple Entente would be replaced by a European Alliance.

Let no one protest that the hatred between the two camps would prevent this. Hate is not a political reality. It is merely a discovery of diplomacy, which creates popular moods in order to cite them as justification for its own errors. Enduring antagonisms exist only in phantasy; there indeed they are carefully cultivated! The present allies [1] have all

[1] This was written early in 1915. — Tr.

waged bitter wars on each other in the course of the past century, and almost all the present opponents have been allies in some previous war. That does not prevent former enemies from standing "shoulder to shoulder" to-day, nor the former allies from fighting each other. Already we in Germany hear talk of the possibility of an alliance with one or another of the powers with whom we are at present in bloody combat. There is nothing real to prevent the substitution of a European Alliance for the separate alliances of to-day.

The fact that a general European Alliance need not be political at all, indeed would have no reason to be so, makes such a step easier. If all the nations should unite, there would be no occasion to direct their energies against any other state — unless it be an extra-European constellation. The political aspect would cease to exist, and with it our greatest obstacle would be overcome. A general European Alliance would not have the menacing character of the alliances of the past, and would be far more helpful in economic and social life. Such an agreement would doubtless have its effect upon the political life of the participating states and secure more real protection than the present-day so-called "protective" alliances possibly could. It would also create an atmosphere in which the institutions of the Hague could develop into that which they were intended to be. The Hague Conferences would finally be vivified, and, supported by the will of the organized world, would become effective.

Perhaps the most pressing international problem is that of *over-armament* and its gradual alleviation. It is difficult because it cannot be solved directly but must be dealt with through its underlying causes. Armament is the substitute for order in the prevailing international disorder. It is supposed to defend the body politic just as armor protected the individual in the days of *intra-*national lawlessness. But just as armor was dropped as soon as peace within the nation brought personal security, so armaments will disappear, or at least be decreased, in proportion as international organization does away with international anarchy and achieves national security for its members. The difficulty of the problem vanishes when we understand this indirect method of treatment.

This does not imply that in the face of the fearful burden of armaments we are to fold our hands and fatalistically await the evolution of international organization. In Chapter II I pointed out that the ruinous and futile competition of armaments was created by anarchy and in turn deepened it; indeed that this delirious competition was finally a not inconsiderable cause of the explosion. We must, therefore, not be content to attack the root of the evil by eliminating its known causes: we must treat the symptom as well; for it is constantly becoming more difficult to cure. This is especially necessary since after the war the replacement of armament will give a new incentive to competition in the newest and most effective weapons. The experiences of the war will give a dangerous stimulus to inventors.

Furthermore, the menace of armaments does not consist in their existence or in their size alone, but also in the manner of their disposition and in their mobility. In one way or another, a general and simultaneous reduction is already possible. Here again joint action is an indispensable condition. Isolated action cannot be expected of any one. Finally, a real international control must be looked for. International control of armaments is no longer Utopian. If thereby the possibility of a surprise attack could also be eliminated — an attempt which at best has but small chance of succeeding, then the nations would have this even more valuable security in the bargain.

The reasonable suggestion is often made that the *armament-trade* be taken over by the state, or at least conducted under its very close control. There can be no doubt that the impulse to competitive armament is largely due to the private manufacture of armament, or at least is stimulated and encouraged by it. The intrigues of these huge firms are dangerous not only in that they overburden the economic strength of the population, but also on account of their tremendous resources, and of their international connections, which they use to devise and sharpen controversies. They create the atmosphere which is most favorable to their profits. If the governments manufactured their own arms and ammunition, these disturbing machinations would for the most part disappear. The export of munitions would then be limited; and thus nations would no longer have to increase their armament to protect themselves against countries which they had themselves supplied from their own ammunition factories. The nationalization of the manufacture of armaments would greatly facilitate international control of armaments, and would pave the way for their limitation.

Another crying problem of international fellowship which must be brought nearer to a solution immediately after the war, is that of the *press.*

Who is there who, for years before the war as well as in that critical July week, and in the dark days since, has not turned away with inner shame and open indignation from the performances of that institution which so completely dominates our modern life?

The fact that there is in every country a decent press controlled by men conscious of their duty to the community, simply serves to emphasize the general wretchedness of the situation. We are not here concerned with that respectable press, conscious as it is of its duty, whatever political or national standpoint it may represent. But of those poison factories, those gas-bomb batteries, those gangs of rogues and tavern gamblers who ply their unholy trade in broad daylight, who deceive and defile mankind, slyly pouring the poison of their baseness into heart and head, whose representatives nevertheless pass for honorable men and pose as benefactors in white vests — of that press we must speak.

The inadequacy of diplomacy and the burden of armaments have never done humanity so much harm as has that press. Rank with poison, it grows beneath the very tree of freedom which signifies the deliverance of mankind from the chains of authority. For decades it has excited peoples against one another, has deceived them about each other and has misrepresented the attitude and intentions of them all; it has awakened and constantly cultivated every low instinct, and at the same time with hellish conscientiousness it has blocked the path of those ideas and efforts which might have enlightened and pacified mankind. It sowed hate, distrust and scorn, stirred the wild lust for blood and plunder, until finally it could blow the grand halloo and satisfy its instincts of profit in the flames of world-calamity. All this has happened and is still happening under the mask of patriotism, as a "service to the fatherland"; but all the while the greedy hands behind snatch up the profits of the trade in human beings.

That press is sufficiently well-known. Its owners and their assistants, and the titles of the papers, are named with indignation. There are countries where people have gone so far as publicly to denounce these millionnaire owners as accomplices in the war, and to point to the mountains of dead as the foundations of such fortunes. But those big men known to every one do not stand alone. There is the legion of the little, of the infinitely little, who taken together are dangerous indeed; who, because of their circulation and adaptability to local circumstances, carry the poison into the most remote villages.

I need not go into details to show how this press works, how it spreads its poison, or how it caricatures the spiritual vision of mankind and discredits all the achievements of the human spirit in progress toward internationalism. Mediæval darkness is artificially produced with the most advanced instruments of modern times. It is a case of Ghengis Khan with a telegraph instrument. Detailed description is superfluous, for we all know the evil from our own experience. The phenomena attendant on the war have shown it to be a world-evil more dangerous than all the infernal machines which are preying on humanity on land, on and under the sea, and in the air. No thinking person will any longer dispute that this press is the worst obstacle in the way of permanent peace, real or so-called.

Hence we may hope that as one of the first steps in the restoration of Europe something will be done to free us from this unworthy tyranny. Experience will teach us what instruments are best adapted. All must be tried. Since it is an international evil, much may be expected from coöperative international action. It is doubtful, however, whether legislative measures can accomplish much. But we have learned how to suppress evils like white slavery, pornographic literature and the sale of spirituous liquors, by international legislation; and we can attempt it here, too. In this way the worst grievances can be eliminated. But that would be far from enough. The most effective method seems to me to be thorough enlightenment of the public, a task in which the decent press can coöperate. Gradually the ground can be cut from under the offenders. To boycott such papers and their publishers would certainly be very effective. Respectable papers might assist by refusing to have anything to do with such associates, and by carefully and obviously going a different road. Much might be accomplished by a voluntary international enterprise to name, brand and boycott such sheets. Anything that seems hopeful must be tried. The essential is, to do something. Humanity, which has armed itself to meet pest, cholera, diphtheria, tuberculosis and cancer, will surely find the proper weapon to use against the jingo press.

One of the chief conditions for the restoration and intelligent extension of the European community of nations will be the rapid and successful *removal of the moral rubbish* which the havoc of the world-war will leave behind. There will be other weapons beside those of steel to be silenced. The weapons of the mind, which have caused just as much devastation as have the Mausers and the shrapnel, must also come to rest.

The outbreaks of hate which have occurred on both sides in this war were simply another kind of weapon. They must not be allowed to fight on when the cannon are silenced. *Just as the mines will be removed from the mouths of the rivers and from the seacoasts, so the bombs of hate must be gathered up.* Hate is the propagandist method of the apostles of force and the imperialists. Only in an atmosphere of hate and suspicion can they justify and carry out their ideas. When hostilities have ceased, the task of destroying hate must be begun immediately, and with energy and circumspection.

We cannot, as was done after 1871, trust to the automatic disappearance of hate. We do not want to wait until the generations that have known the war are dead. The restoration of Europe must not be so long postponed. The convulsion was so mighty, the destruction so tremendous, that delay might make the evil incurable. The best chance for salvation is in losing no time. Ours is a rescue-work of the first importance. It is not enough to repair the visible damages of war by providing more care for invalids, by building orphan asylums and homes for the blind or by giving aid to widows; nor by glorifying war in monuments and halls of fame. More important than all these is that preventive action which will make it possible for the suffering peoples to meet again as human beings and in a manner worthy of human beings. Upon that is dependent the coöperation of the citizens of all civilized nations, and with it the salvation of mankind.

The task will surely be lighter than after the last great European war. The aftermath of this war will be too awful; and we better understand why great nations are so stiff-necked in their antagonisms. Had France and Germany understood each other, the world-war would not have come. The task will be easier because the war could not destroy what pacifism had achieved toward such international understanding. Destructive though it be, the war cannot demolish the foundations of our decades of careful work. We may expect that the work of reconciliation, previously so well organized, will be resumed immediately after the war, and that it will not require complete reorganization. That will be a great advantage; for people from every country, stirred by the sights and horrors of war, will join us, eager to serve in the great campaign for the elimination of hate. A *League of Europeans* will arise, — not an association with a programme and statutes, but a free union of those who, aching with their own wounds, understand the anguish of the age and are ready to relieve it. This League of Europeans will consist of those men and women who have come to understand that the evils of war poison life even when the cannon are silent, and that they can only be overcome by an understanding which knows no national borderlines, and with the coöperation of all nations. Its members will be those who feel it their duty to forget their own pain and their own gaping wounds for the service of that which is above all nations, humanity. The civic heroism of peaceful activity will be manifest in their activity. They will be scorned and scolded, accused of lack of patriotism and of Utopianism. And yet they will be the true patriots and the truly practical politicians.

The number of international problems whose solution awaits the organization of the European nations is infinite. Only a few of those which most affect the weal and woe of our time could be considered here. We have done nothing but call attention to them. When the war is past, work will be resumed in the arsenals of peace, and the happy time will come when all these problems are to be solved and the foundation laid for a new humanity. *Most fundamental of all problems is that of establishing international justice.* Its course may be traced through all the affairs of men. We have not spoken of it directly, but all that has been said here has been meant as a contribution to the fulfilment of this great demand. Justice is the foundation of nations, and the community of nations can have no other foundation. It is the happiness of nations. Its absence has been the cause of their sorrow.

European history of the last century, since the convulsions of the Napoleonic era, has been governed by two principles, one following the other. They are the principles of legitimacy and of nationality. The first collapsed in the storm of revolution; the latter is collapsing under the strain of world-catastrophe to-day. A new principle is arising to dominate European history, which for the first time will give princes and peoples complete enjoyment of their rights: it is the new, the constructive, safeguarding and liberating *principle of International Justice.*

CHAPTER VI

THE COÖPERATIVE UNION OF EUROPE

IN the previous chapter we saw under what conditions the organization of Europe might be extended. We pointed out that a selfish interest in organization was a surer bond than compulsion. Attention was called to the fact that no artificial construction was to be considered, but rather the development of the germs of organization already at hand. Europe must grow into the new community, just as in the past it grew into anarchy. The old historic units must be combined, not as parts of a federation, but rather as independent members of a great union created for a specific purpose. It is true that war is a political phenomenon, but it would be false to assume that the organization which is to supersede it must therefore be of a political nature. On the contrary, experience demonstrates that political unions such as our present-day alliances finally lead to war. If our purpose is to promote the association of states for the furtherance of their numerous non-political common interests, we shall meet less opposition than if we attempt simultaneously to organize them politically. In the long run a close association in economic, technical, social and ideal fields will inevitably make itself felt in political relations as well. Following the line of least resistance, there will eventually be a complete form of international organization.

If this war, as appears to be the case, demonstrates the impracticability of the old notions of subjugation, and if at the same time the realization grows that in Europe, with its confusion of politics and nationalities, federation is impracticable, then the idea of such association will triumph. It will be clear that Europe is not going to become Cossack by conquest nor Republican by federation, and that its future lies rather on the diagonal of these forces. It is a "*Coöperative*

Union" (*Zweckverband*) which promises the solution. The conception is a compromise; it overcomes obstacles that would interfere with any other plan. The name indicates that in such a union, without sacrificing the independence of the participants, certain specified interests can be better represented by common action. The states are not to be sacrificed to any final purpose, as in the case of a political federation; rather the purpose shall be service to the states. They will no longer aspire to solve their problems individually, by the method which has so often led them to dissipate their energies in futile struggle against one another; but coöperatively, with great economy of effort and energy, they will meet the difficulties — which in most cases will cease to be such simply because of the joint action of the interested parties.

The Coöperative Union of Europe, even before the war, had ceased to be a mere demand. It already existed in a number of bipartite and general international agree-

THE COÖPERATIVE UNION 137

ments, and in various international bureaus and commissions. Many matters of transportation, commerce, civil law, police, science, social policy and agriculture were already internationally regulated.[1]

These international agreements and the various international activities to which they gave rise constituted a beginning of an *international administration.*[2] But they lacked unity — there was no centralization. They had arisen mechanically in response to changed conditions, and there had never been any deliberate far-seeing organization of them. The age of anarchy had not the power for such an achievement. When the war is over the time will have come to develop those institutions and to organize them with the definite purpose of meeting the demands of the international situation. Thus the Coöperative Union of Europe will find its foundation already laid.

---

[1] For further information on this subject see my "Handbuch der Friedensbewegung," 2d edition, vol. 2, p. 269.

[2] See Chapter II, p. 51.

There will be no lack of matters which can be made subject to international regulation and administration. New matters will very soon be added to the list of those already so administered.[1] Our economic, cultural and social needs are already common to all nations. The war has not changed the situation; nor has the belief, so common in the first excitement, that internationalism had collapsed. When normal conditions are restored, the imperative necessity of international coöperation will again be evident. The "Coöperative Union" will meet certain general international problems which in the past have received special treatment in each individual case. Its great importance for Europe will be that it will become the organ of the states in all these common interests. For the first time *Europe will have a central bureau for her common interests*, and thus for the first time Europe will be more than

[1] The possibility of adjusting the great commercial conflicts may be mentioned. Internationalization of markets as well as of the highways leading to them would certainly be a praiseworthy task for the Coöperative Union.

THE COÖPERATIVE UNION 139

a mere geographical expression. However trivial its activity may at first be, and however difficult the procedure, once it is established, Europe will never again be able to dispense with it. It will give Europe solidity and cohesion, and the promise of yet more for the future.

The creation of such a Coöperative Union would not be without precedent. Such an institution has existed for more than a quarter of a century in the western hemisphere, in the *Pan-American Union*, which, rather than the constitutional form of the United States, is adapted to serve as a model for the new European Union. In 1889 eighteen American republics met in the first Pan-American Conference. There had been agitation for such a union ever since 1810. This continental congress has met four times. The fifth conference was to have been held in November, 1914, but was postponed on account of the war. The Pan-American Union led to the establishment in Washington of the *Pan-American Bureau*, which is supported by the twenty-one republics. The Administrative Board of this international bureau is composed of the accredited diplomatic representatives in Washington of the various American republics, and the Secretary of State of the United States presides.[1]

The discussions and decisions of the conferences cover the whole field of the extra-political relations of the American republics. They have to do with the regulation and extension of railways and of navigation, of tariff problems, of harbor rights, of consular affairs, coinage, weights and measures, sanitation, regulations for aliens, extradition; further, the regulation of civil law, patent rights and copyrights, scientific enterprises and the conclusion of arbitration treaties. An extensive programme for the furtherance of international intercourse by means of exchange professors and scholars, travel, promotion of instruction in languages, etc., has been undertaken. Especial attention has been paid to

[1] See my "Pan-Amerika. Entwicklung, Umfang und Bedeutung der Pan-Amerikanischen Bewegung (1810–1910)." Berlin, 1910.

THE COÖPERATIVE UNION 141

the encouragement of trade and commerce by exchange of information, by expositions and museums of commerce.

It will occasion no surprise that Pan-Americanism, despite its purely economic and social programme, has reacted upon political life as well. Years of peaceful coöperation between nations and their representatives strengthen confidence, engender a habit of mind which does not presuppose hostile intentions in one's neighbors, and in critical issues reënforces the determination to let rational considerations decide. Arbitration and mediation have reached their highest development on the American continents. The peaceful coöperative union expedites peaceful settlement of such disputes as inevitably arise.

Pan-Americanism is not only a model for Europe; it is a warning as well. Before the war there was much talk of the *American menace*, by which was meant economic competition. It exists; but in a different form. A continent so organized will only too easily win precedence over divided Europe. If that disorganization which has led to war should continue after the war, the danger of the associated states of Pan-America outstripping Europe will be far greater. The war has changed the relative position of Europe and America, and not to the advantage of Europe. Europe will lag behind America because of its disorganization, and also because of its exhaustion. Hence a Coöperative Union must be formed, that a united Europe may meet that united continent across the ocean — not for attack, but to make further coöperation possible.

The Pan-European Union need not slavishly follow the American model. It should be adapted to the peculiar conditions of Europe. Since the relations between the European states are livelier than those between the American republics and since they are so much closer to each other, since their interests are more complicated and the possibilities of conflict more abundant, a conference meeting only once in every four or six

THE COÖPERATIVE UNION 143

years would not amount to much. The assemblies should occur at least every three years. In the meantime there should be a *Pan-European Bureau* — a central organ for the Union — exercising wide powers in coöperation with the permanent delegates of the various governments. This bureau should have its seat in the capital or in a leading city of a neutral European country. While the Hague Conferences and the Hague Bureau would develop the legal relations of the nations, the Pan-European Bureau and the Pan-European Conferences would control the extension and regulation of international relations in actual practice.

Such coöperation in the practical necessities of life would soon react upon *political life*. Despite the independence of the individual states — or perhaps on account of it — the Pan-European Union would not be without influence on the political constitution of the continent. Continuous coöperation would emphasize the economic and cultural interdependence on the old continent, and in time political differences would lose some of their menacing character, and means of reconciliation would quite easily be found. A condition favorable to the effectiveness of the Hague machinery would thus be created. Such coöperation would strengthen legal coöperation, and create that will to law, the absence of which has condemned the Hague tribunal to impotence. A European Union is at present more desirable than a worldwide one, especially in view of these political consequences. The European states must first become accustomed to coöperation in their own European affairs without complicating them with world-considerations. Where broader matters are at issue, these can best be settled as before by worldwide conferences or through those international bureaus which already exist. Often the coöperation of the Pan-American and the Pan-European Unions will be necessary, and it may be taken for granted that such a Pan-European Union would finally develop into a *World-Union* (*Weltzweckverband*). But we should begin at the beginning.

THE COÖPERATIVE UNION

It is highly desirable that all the European states take part. The isolation of one of the great powers or of a group of powers would not make it entirely impracticable, but it would limit its effectiveness and permit the suspicion, to which past European history would give only too much support, that the Union was directed against some particular nation. That would be quite contrary to the spirit of the organization. The Union should be directed neither against Russia nor against England, against the central powers or the western powers, but solely against the old Europe and its heedlessness, its bitterness, its hate and anarchy. Its service should be to promote the creation of an organized, a coöperative, a self-conscious new Europe.

CHAPTER VII

THE PACIFISM OF YESTERDAY AND OF TO-MORROW

THERE are two books whose titles hamper the progress of pacifism. The titles only are dangerous — not the books. Just because Kant's "Eternal Peace" and Bertha von Suttner's "Lay Down Your Arms" have had so wide a circulation, many have thought it unnecessary to know their contents, and have been content to accept the wording of their titles as the programme of pacifism. Accordingly eternal peace and general disarmament appeared to be our programme. This has hurt the pacifist movement, but it has hurt even more those who have been misled by such superficiality. It kept them from appreciating those demands of the age to which we called their attention.

When, then, the war broke out, such superficial and infatuated thinkers held but *one* opinion: that pacifism had failed and was proved an illusion. To have disarmed would have been madness, and the dream of eternal peace was ended. As if we had ever dreamed such a dream, or had ever pleaded for disarmament! Such people were not disturbed by the facts of the case; there were the two titles! A person who defined Darwinism to-day as the descent of man from the ape, or who defined Socialism as the redistribution of all property, would hardly be called educated. But a similar pronouncement about pacifism, eternal peace and disarmament does not yet carry the same stigma. There are still people with high-sounding scientific titles who believe that there is such a pacifism, who *so* explain its aims, and undertake to refute it with such cheap allegations.

The war has brought no collapse of pacifism. It is the collapse of that "practical" policy which scorned to accept the pacifists' suggestions for self-preservation. It is European diplomacy and the apostles of force, the fanatics of preparedness and the Utopians of world-domination, who are bankrupt — they who before had to wait for the war accepting the cold hard facts. They are bankrupt, as I have tried to show in the preceding chapters — they who lived in the belief that peace could be secured by preparing for war and only by preparing for war; they who thought that a sharp sword and dry powder outweighed all the instruments of reconciliation and peaceful settlement. Rivers of blood and the desolation of war have proved this philosophy unfitted for the age.

The opponents and critics who thought pacifism was living in the clouds were mistaken. To pacifists the war brought no disillusionment. Just because they had seen it coming, they had struggled to prevent it, and sounded the warning. They indicated the path of reason which might have avoided it. Had they been as sure of world-peace as these others believed them to be, they would have ceased their agitation. It would have been superfluous. Pacifists never indulged in the dream that they who fed the fires of national hatred would escape without war. They merely demanded that the instruments of compromise and conciliation be strengthened, so that hate and jingoism might be stifled and disputes be settled by the instruments of reason. They failed in their endeavor; but the results of their failure are the proof that the salvation of the future lies in the success of their programme.

In the first chapter I pointed out that the pacifists years ago diagnosed the situation correctly, and foresaw that international anarchy must end in explosion. Only a few weeks before the outbreak of the war, in early June, when very few appreciated the delicacy of the situation, when the Austro-Hungarian Foreign Minister, Count Berchtold, was still honorary president of the Twenty-First World Peace Congress that was to have been held at Vienna in the fall, and before the crime of Serajevo had been committed, I wrote an article entitled *"Operation, or Medical Treatment?"* for the *"Friedens-Warte."* It appeared in the last number issued before the war. I referred to the general feeling that things in Europe could not long continue as they then were. I expressed the fear that this sentiment might force the militarists of all nations to attempt to solve the complicated situation by the sword. I called that a desperate method. "This is perhaps one of the most dangerous moments in the history of our continent," I wrote early in June, 1914. "Dangerous because desperation may force the decision, and at such times reason loses its power." I saw the desire to operate, and suggested medical treatment of the evil instead. "Operation might improve the situation," I said; "the fires of hell, once let loose, might consume everything that could serve to revivify the madness of militarism. Out of that operation might come forth a new life without those anachronisms which to-day obstruct the evolution of the continent. The clash might realize the organization of the world and the domination of law." Nevertheless I advised the peaceful method of medical treatment. Eight weeks later Europe was aflame. Those who play with the trite phrases about pacifism to-day, who call us "visionaries," "blown away" by events which were a "tremendous disillusionment" to us, would do well to read that article — and a hundred other articles by our comrades in this and other countries. They would learn how well aware we were of the critical nature of that "peace" whose character we sought to change.

The following paragraph which I take at random from her "Marginal Notes to Current History" will show how *Bertha von Suttner* felt — she whom our opponents call fortunate because supposedly her opportune death kept her from a great disillusionment. It was written just ten years ago, in 1905:

". . . It is high time for this federation of Europe. With all the tinder that is being fanned between the nations, with the madness that is blowing over us from the East, *peace cannot be maintained much longer;* it must be secured, *i.e.* Europe must be organized. . . ."

On the 12th of February, 1914, when we were engaged in preparations for the Vienna Peace Congress, she wrote prophetically in her diary: "The newspaper war between Austria and Russia is already in full swing. Perhaps war will break out and make the Congress impossible."

It cannot be denied that this war would have been no disillusionment to Bertha von Suttner. Painful indeed — it was painful to all pacifists,to all forward-looking men. But it was not the surprise it seems to have been to those who began to think about pacifism only after the war had broken out, but who had scoffed at it when they might have been of some avail.

No, the war was *no surprise* to us. We knew that it might have been avoided, and we struggled loyally for that end. Our ideas had begun to influence politics, and the achievements of international reconciliation grew every day. The hope arose that the great crisis might be passed, and that the people of Europe might without a bloody

PACIFISM — PAST AND FUTURE

struggle arrive at a settlement promising peace and harmony for the future. But the forces of international anarchy were too strong. The war came before our ideas had won full sway. Now it must complete what we had not yet achieved. Its brutal method of instruction may perhaps be more successful.

We pacifists were misrepresented both in regard to the extent of our hopes and to the instruments by which we hoped to attain them. We were accused of the crudest attitude toward the complicated problem of *disarmament* — the first impulse to the investigation and study of which had been given by us. It was said that we sought disarmament, even one-sided disarmament of our own people, while the other nations were still in armor. Disarmament was made to appear the fundament of our teachings. Such is the curse of those familiar titles, "Lay Down Your Arms" and "Eternal Peace." Nothing was further from our minds than such an attempt to begin a house with the roof. We looked forward to a general and simultaneous relief from the burden of armaments as the final consequence of that reorganization of international relations which we urged.

We were misrepresented on other subjects as well. We were said to regard *arbitration* as a universal remedy, which would solve the most difficult problems. In reality we looked upon it as only one among many peaceful methods of adjustment. This was another case where a problem, the study of which had developed into a great science, was stated with the crudest simplicity. It was not we who were guilty of that misrepresentation, but the naïveté of our opponents who did not observe that we understood that not all international conflicts were capable of legal solution, and that the character of these disputes would have to be changed before they would be capable of such solution. Our critics had no conception of the problem of transforming international anarchy into international organization, or of the change in the character of international disputes thus to be effected. They knew nothing of the fundamental problem of pacifism. In their heads buzzed only the two phrases, disarmament and eternal peace.

They were equally ignorant of the *extent of pacifism*. They had no fineness of perception; they could only see things in lumps: here an evil, there a remedy. Of the great work of education, of the gradual diffusion of ideas with the purpose of gradual transformation of an evil into a rational state of affairs, they noticed nothing. In how many fields of human activity pacifism makes itself felt to-day — often without its agents being aware of the pacifist origin or the pacifist purpose of their activity! Has not every political party, every religious confession, every school of thought, accepted at least a part of the pacifist programme or in some fashion undertaken pacifist activities — often indeed so unconsciously that they thought that they were opposing organized pacifism? Has not all the work of the world become pacifist in purpose, do not the sciences of international law, economics and sociology emphasize their pacifist elements, have not entirely new sciences such as the Science of Internationalism (*Internationalogie*) and the Economics of Human Life (*Menschen-ökonomie*) arisen as a result of the pacifist movement? Its radius of action is far greater than the horizon of those who scorn and misunderstand it. Its teachings permeate every field of human activity, and every kind of activity serves its purposes. In roundabout ways, but comprehensively and certainly, it draws near its goal.

In the turmoil of the war we are told to unlearn and learn anew. It will be easier to renounce old errors when to have believed them carries no stigma. Good! Let us revise our views, adapt them to reality, and then meet life with them. Pacifism expects such a revision on the part of its opponents who have been so guilty of misunderstanding and misrepresentation. Pacifism does not need to unlearn. Perhaps alone in this time of general collapse, it needs no such revision. *Its great hour has come.* When humanity awakens from this bloody hallucination, when it sees and counts and realizes the cost of all the harvest of war, when it is able coolly to distinguish between cause and effect, means and end — then humanity will and must return to the doctrines offered it so long ago by this despised pacifism.

The hour draws near. In millions of minds the world over the thought arises, and the fateful question is put: Was it inevitable? Must it be thus eternally? And the answer swells to an iron echo, awakening and sweeping the world: NO!

The past can no longer be revised, but the future is in our hands. The age that is dawning is the age of peace, the great era of restoration, of knowledge taught by bloody experience, of reconciliation and adjustment, the age of the funeral celebration for this last tremendous sacrifice to human aberration, the great age, foreseen by us and prepared with our heart's blood, the era of

THE RESTORATION OF EUROPE.

Printed in the United States of America.

THE following pages contain advertisements of a few of the Macmillan books on kindred subjects.

The European Anarchy

By G. LOWES DICKINSON

Cloth, $1.00

Mr. Dickinson's book gives in broad outline a just estimate of the European concept of government — what he calls the European Anarchy — with particular reference to the underlying causes of the war and the possibility of a movement toward better things in the future. The key-note of the discussion is Germany, her expansion and her desire for future expansion, what was legitimate in it and what was disastrous, the influence of Bismarck, and Bismarck's success in divorcing from the German mind the old, generous idealism of 1848 in favor of a Machiavellianism as far removed from the real needs of human nature as any romanticism could be. Mr. Dickinson recognizes that the fundamental interests of the European nations demand a united Europe, and wherever he criticizes the past, it is only with the searching hope of reconstruction for the future.

THE MACMILLAN COMPANY

Publishers   64-66 Fifth Avenue   New York

The Diplomacy of the Great War

By ARTHUR BULLARD

Cloth, 12mo, $1.50

A book which contributes to an understanding of the war by revealing something of the diplomatic negotiations that preceded it. The author gives the history of international politics in Europe since the Congress of Berlin in 1878, and considers the new ideals that have grown up about the function of diplomacy during the last generation, so that the reader is in full possession of the general trend of diplomatic development. There is added a chapter of constructive suggestions in respect to the probable diplomatic settlements resulting from the war, and a consideration of the relations between the United States and Europe.

THE MACMILLAN COMPANY
Publishers   64–66 Fifth Avenue   New York

OUR NATIONAL PROBLEMS

The Heritage of Tyre
By WILLIAM BROWN MELONEY

Once our flag was known in every port and our keels traversed every sea; all the whalers of the world came out of New Bedford then, and, "Salem" on a ship's stern was as familiar a sight as "Liverpool" is to-day. The Yankee clippers will never come back, but William Brown Meloney shows how we can restore the stars and stripes to the seven seas and the prestige of the world's greatest merchant marine to the American people.

"An opportunity to recover our sea heritage stands forth," he writes, "an opportunity of half a world at war — such an opportunity as, in all likelihood, will never present itself again under similar circumstances. We are at peace, we have the necessary maritime genius, we have in abundance the natural resources, to found and maintain a merchant marine. Either we shall seize this opportunity forthwith, or else our sea folly of the past will continue a hostage to the future, to be delivered only, if at all, by the edge of a crimson sword." *50 cents*

The Forks of the Road
By WASHINGTON GLADDEN

Can a nation lead except by war? That is the question which faces the United States to-day. Two paths are open, and Washington Gladden has written a book forcefully stating his conviction of which we must choose. Our example is of greater value than our threats; our position demands that we stand firm for peace. The author points out that the present universal desire for peace, expressed in the utterances of every nation, the ultimate beliefs of every religion, the hope and prayer of every individual, needs a leader in the church and an exponent in America.

"If each nation insists on continuing to be a law unto itself and on making its own interests supreme and paramount, the natural reactions will ensue, retribution will repeat itself, and the same dreadful harvesting — only more dire and more universal — will be ready for the reaper before the end of another generation." *50 cents*

THE MACMILLAN COMPANY
Publishers   64-66 Fifth Avenue   **New York**

OUR NATIONAL PROBLEMS

The Pentecost of Calamity

By OWEN WISTER

"One of the most striking and moving utterances. . . . Let all Americans read it." — *The Congregationalist.*

"It is written with sustained charm and freshness of insight." — *New York Times.*

"It is a flaming thing, itself a tongue of Pentecost." — *Boston Advertiser.*

"Mr. Wister's artistic power at its best." — *Philadelphia Ledger.*

"A strong book which sets out to be just a passionate plea to America to find its own soul." — Rabbi STEPHEN S. WISE.

"In 'The Pentecost of Calamity' Owen Wister sees and speaks as a prophet. With rare spiritual insight and sympathy he penetrates to the real meaning of the world tragedy under whose shadow we are living. I am glad we have an American writer able to speak the voiceless longing of an awakened world." — Rev. CHARLES A. EATON, Pastor of the Madison Avenue Baptist Church.

50 cents

Their True Faith and Allegiance

By GUSTAVUS OHLINGER

"True culture demands neither a press agent nor a conscious propaganda. . . . Viewed in the light of history, the propaganda of those Germans who are only geographically and politically Americans is as unnatural as it is pernicious. . . . Under these influences an American nation would be impossible, and without an American nation the American state would succumb to disintegration. . . . It is for those Germans who fought under Schurz and Sigel in the Civil War, to rebuke these false prophets and to turn the aspirations of their countrymen in the direction of true American nationalism." — *Their True Faith and Allegiance.*

50 cents

THE MACMILLAN COMPANY

Publishers   64-66 Fifth Avenue   New York